Raw Transitions
My Raw Magic Month
A 28 Day Menu Plan

By
Kate Magic

First published in the UK by Raw Living Publications 2020

First edition

Copyright ©Kate Magic 2020

Layout and design: Simon Earl

Cover design: Carlotta Raimondi

Back cover photo: Bridie O'Sullivan

Recipe photography: Kate Magic

No reproduction without permission. All rights reserved. No part of this publication may be reproduced, stored in, or introduced into a retrieval system, copied, or transmitted by any form or any means – electronically, photocopy, recording or otherwise, without the permission of the copyright owners.

The right of Kate Magic to be asserted as author of this work has been asserted in accordance with Sections 77 of the Copyright, Designs and Patents act 1988.

Raw Living Publications

23 Ford Rd, Totnes, Devon, TQ9 5LE

Printed and bound in the UK by Acanthus Press.

ISBN: 978-1-9161381-1-7

Contents

How to Follow 5
Raw Basics 6
Menu Schedule 8
My Raw Magic Month 10
Week One 16
Week Two 26
Week Three 34
Week Four 41
Transitional Support 50
Mylk Recipes 56
Green Juice Recipes 58
Breakfast Recipes 60
Lunch Recipes 62
Dinner Recipes 72
Snacks 86
Equipment lists 89
Shopping lists 90
Resources 95

How to Follow

Welcome to what I hope will be the beginning of a wonderful new relationship with your food and your body. I've tried to keep this as simple as possible for you, because I believe the simpler something is, the more effective it is.

This plan starts you off on a high percentage raw vegan diet for the first week, leading to an 80% raw vegan diet on the second week, and a fully raw vegan diet for weeks three and four. I myself have been on a raw vegan diet for 30 years, as well as raising three sons into adulthood on these kind of menus, so I have a wealth of experience in making raw food nutritionally sustaining, easy to prepare, and irresistibly delicious. There are a handful of nutritional guidelines you will find on the next page that my programme follows. In a nutshell, I believe that:

- Hydration is key, and our liquid intake is just as important as our solid intake.
- Healthy fats are the foundation of a healthy diet and on a raw food diet an abundance of healthy fats are essential for adequate calorific intake.
- Alkaline foods such as leafy greens are preferable over acidic foods such as meat, grains and dairy
- Low sugar is also a vital component of health, so although you will find plenty of desserts and treats on the menu, none of them are overly sweet.

I've got you on three meals a day; breakfast, lunch and dinner, plus recipes for daily Mylks, juices and teas, and snacks. This is not a deprivation diet in any way; my intention is to keep you so full with wonderful raw food that you won't be craving anything else.

In this handbook, firstly you have the menu plan for you to easily refer to (Pages 8-9). Following that is the menu plan broken down into detail (Pages 16-49) – this is where to look when you're stuck about something. Next we have over 60 recipes (Pages 56-88) that will have you and anyone you're sharing them with 'oohing' and 'aahing' with delight. I've kept all the recipes as easy as I can, because I know you've probably got too much going on to be in the kitchen for hours every day. Then finally, at the back (Pages 90-94), we have the ingredients lists. Making sure you have everything you need in is key, and getting the best quality, freshest ingredients will make all the difference to how your meals turn out.

So, short of going to the shops and cooking it for you (which you know I actually would do if I had the time), I've done everything I can to make your experimentations with raw foods as successful as possible. Have fun!

Raw Basics

The Magic Plate

Key principles to create a solid foundation of cellular health.

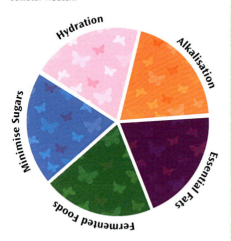

Hydration – minimum 3 litres liquids a day, can include medicinal teas, plant-based Mylks, juices, fermented drinks, coconut water, activated water.

Alkalisation – aim to consume around 70% alkalizing foods in a day. Include plenty of leafy greens, green juices and green powders.

Essential Fats – include an abundance of healthy fats – nuts, seeds, avocados, olives, coconut, cacao and their respective oils.

Include **Fermented Foods** & drinks every day to cultivate a healthy biome.

Minimise Sugars, even fruit sugars feed disease and unbalance insulin levels. Get your fuel from fats, not carbs.

Optimum Raw Vegan Diet

Elements necessary to successfully sustain the diet in the Northern European climate. (Percentage is by quantity on the plate, not calorific intake).

50% Vegetables, pref organic, local and seasonal. Making vegetables the basis of your diet is more important than whether you eat them raw or cooked.

50% from the following food groups

(balance will vary from individual to individual but make sure they are all staples in your diet).

Fruits

Nuts & Seeds

Sprouted pulses, seeds & Microgreens

Fermented Vegetables

Sea Vegetables

Superfoods

Top Rules of Raw

- There is some dispute over the exact temperature that a food stops being technically "raw", but it's somewhere between 40-50 deg C. Above this temperature, the enzymes are destroyed, and enzymes are the life-force of food. So eat alive to feel alive.

- Start at 50% raw. Plenty of people do 50% and feel great on it. Many people work up to around 70% over time, but very few sustain over 90%, and 100% is a bit of a myth.

- To build up the immune system, include raw at every meal, and eat the raw foods first, or alongside the cooked component of the meal (not afterwards).

- Consistency is key. Set yourself realistic goals that you can maintain, rather than unachievable targets that create a yo-yo effect. Better to make small changes steadily over a longer period of time than rush in headlong and then give up because it's too much too soon.

- Keep it simple. The body responds best to simple messages. The more unprocessed and unadulterated your food, the happier your body will be.

- Focus on what you can do. This is a diet of inclusion, not exclusion. Focus on all the exciting new foods you want to try and recipes you want to make, rather than keep thinking about what you are trying to cut out.

- Just as important as what you eat are: exercise, rest, time in nature, mindfulness, living with purpose, and cultivating effective de-stressing techniques that work for you.

Menu Schedule

DAY	MORNING PREP	TEA	BREAKFAST	LUNCH	SNACK	DINNER	PRE-PREP
DAY 1	SOAK ALMONDS	REISHI & GOJI TEA	CEREAL	RICE CAKES	RAW CHOC	SALAD & BAKED SWEET POTATO	MAKE RAW CHOCOLATE
				GUACAMOLE			MAKE CEREAL
				ROCKET			MAKE CHIA COOKIES
				CRUDITÉS			
DAY 2	SOAK ARAME	GINGER & GOJI TEA	CEREAL	OATCAKES	CHIA COOKIES	ARAME & QUINOA SALAD	
	SOAK CHIA			TURMERIC BUTTER			
				ALFALFA SPROUTS			
				CUCUMBER			
DAY 3		ETERNITEEA	CEREAL	NORI ROLLS	TRAIL MIX	MILLET & SPINACH SALAD	
DAY 4	SOAK FLAX	INFINITEEA	CEREAL	MILLET & SPINACH SALAD	RAW CHOC	TEMPEH STIR FRY	
DAY 5	SOAK HEMP	LEMON GINGER & GOJI	CEREAL	HUMMUS	CHIA COOKIES	TAHINI KALE SALAD & ROASTED VEGGIES	MAKE BREAD
				CORN CHIPS			
				CRUDITÉS			
DAY 6		GYNOSTEMMA GINGER & GOJI	CEREAL	STUFFED AVO	TRAIL MIX	REUBEN'S TOMATO SOUP & AUTHENTIC BREAD	MAKE CANDY
				RICE CAKES OR OAT CAKES			KALE CHIPS
DAY 7	SOAK HAZELNUTS	SCHIZANDRA & GOJI TEA	CEREAL	KALE CHIPS	CANDY	FREE DINNER NIGHT	BLUEBERRY PIE
				TOMATO SALAD			
DAY 8		REISHI & GOJI TEA	CEREAL	REPEAT YOUR FAVOURITE	BLUEBERRY PIE	REPEAT YOUR FAVOURITE	CHIA PORRIDGE
DAY 9		GINGER & GOJI TEA	CHIA PORRIDGE	NORI ROLLS	RAW CHOCOLATE	ROASTED PARSNIPS & ROCKET SALAD	CRACKERS
DAY 10		ETERNITEEA	CHIA PORRIDGE	TURMERIC BUTTER & CRACKERS	CANDY	PASTA IN A RAW SAUCE	
DAY 11		INFINITEEA	CHIA PORRIDGE	GUACAMOLE WRAPS	TRAIL MIX	SPINACH & POTATO CURRY	HUMMUS
							MAKE MORE CHIA PORRIDGE
DAY 12		LEMON GINGER & GOJI	CHIA PORRIDGE	RAW HUMMUS CRUDITÉS OLIVES	BLUEBERRY PIE	STEAMED BROCCOLI & COLESLAW	BAYONNAISE

DAY	MORNING PREP	TEA	BREAKFAST	LUNCH	SNACK	DINNER	PRE-PREP
DAY 13		GYNOSTEMMA GINGER & GOJI	CHIA PORRIDGE	BAYONNAISE CRACKERS	CANDY	THAI YELLOW CURRY	PUMPKIN PÂTÉ
DAY 14		SCHIZANDRA & GOJI TEA	CHIA PORRIDGE	PUMPKIN SEED WRAPS	RAW CHOCOLATE	FREE DINNER NIGHT	MAKE SHORTBREAD
DAY 15			CHIA PORRIDGE	REPEAT YOUR FAVOURITE	SHORTBREAD	STUFFED AVO & SPINACH SALAD	
DAY 16			CHIA PORRIDGE	HEMP TABBOULEH	BLUEBERRY PIE	INSTANT PIZZA	MAKE FALAFEL SOAK OATS
DAY 17			OATS	SUNSHINE SOUP	CHIA COOKIES	FALAFEL & HEMP TABBOULEH	SOAK OATS
DAY 18			OATS	SUSHI	CANDY	COURGETTE NOODLES IN MARINARA	TACOS SOAK OATS
DAY 19			OATS	CUCUMBER SALAD & CAULIFLOWER CHEESE	TRAIL MIX	NORI TACOS	SOAK OATS
DAY 20			OATS	MEDITERRANEAN SALAD	SHORTBREAD	UMAMI KALE & KELP NOODLEs	YOUR FAVOURITE RAW DESSERT SOAK OATS
DAY 21			OATS	SAUERKRAUT SLAW	RAW CHOCOLATE	CAULIFLOWER RICE & CURRY	SOAK OATS
DAY 22			OATS	REPEAT YOUR FAVOURITE	CHIA COOKIES	YOUR FAVOURITE DESSERT REPEAT YOUR FAVOURITE	CRACKERS & CHOC SPREAD MUHAMMARA
DAY 23			CRACKERS & CHOC SPREAD	MUHAMMARA	BLUEBERRY PIE	BEET IT SOUP	
DAY 24			CRACKERS & CHOC SPREAD	SANDWICHES	SHORTBREAD	KALE CAESAR SALAD	
DAY 25			CRACKERS & CHOC SPREAD	KIMCHI SALAD	CANDY	SEA SPAGETTI & PESTO	STUFFED PEPPERS
DAY 26			CRACKERS & CHOC SPREAD	CARROT & SPINACH SOUP	TRAIL MIX	SUNFLOWER STUFFED PEPPERS	
DAY 27			CRACKERS & CHOC SPREAD	WRAWPS	RAW CHOCOLATE	INSTANT KELP NOODLES	PREPARE FOR THE FEAST
DAY 28			CRACKERS & CHOC SPREAD	RAMEN	BLUEBERRY PIE	FEAST	

My Raw Magic Month Easy Menu Plan

I truly believe doing raw foods is easy and fun. Making food that is delicious as it is nutritious is something that comes instinctively to me, and I don't see any reason why it can't come instinctively to you as well, once you've had a little guidance in the right direction. Eating the best food the planet has to offer, on every level, should be something we can do every day. For me personally, nourishing myself in this way fills me with so much joy, and feeling this vitality in my body, clarity in my mind, and lightness in my heart, is a pleasure I wish everyone could experience.

I've created this menu plan to hold your hand for a full 28 days as you transition into a high raw diet. Whether you sustain it for longer or not doesn't matter, because I've created a gentle and practical detox programme that helps your body adjust gradually. As it's not extreme like a juice fast, you're much less likely to lapse, and if you do, the side effects won't be so dramatic. All the information you need should be in these pages, but if you're finding something particularly tricky, don't forget you can book a consult with me so we can sort your issues out.

The most important thing to bear in mind with this programme is to individualise it to suit your own needs and tastes. You can stick to it like a Bible if you choose, but I'd rather you didn't!

I'm going to break down the rules from which it's important not to deviate, but other than that, if there's something on the menu that you love and you want to repeat it, great, go ahead. If there's something that you don't like and you want to skip it, no worries.

As often as possible, I've tried to give you options. So if you don't have a dehydrator, it should be easy to buy that item pre-packaged. If an item is expensive to purchase, I've given you a budget alternative.

The only equipment you need is a good blender. If you have a dehydrator and have the time to be dehydrating yourself, that's going to save you a lot of money.

If you're having cravings for certain foods that you can't ignore, then eat and enjoy those foods, but try and stick to the programme as well. For maximum benefits, try and be fully raw for the last 14 days, but if you can't do it, don't beat yourself up about it, just eat as much raw food on top of the cooked fare as you can.

After you've completed the 28 days, I recommend going back down to a diet similar to week one again. If you like you could start the programme all over again. But if you can at least sustain the week one diet, you're winning.

I've included shopping lists for each day, and reminders of where you need to be soaking and sprouting in advance. Eating this way does require a little organization and forward-planning, but that shouldn't be a problem with your new-found energy and mental focus!

The basic premise of raw foods is to eat foods in which the enzymes have not been destroyed by heat. Enzymes are like the life-force energy in food, so when we eat raw, we feel more alive. It's debatable at what temperature the enzymes are destroyed, but it's somewhere around 45 deg C. Enzyme-depleted food also puts more strain on the immune system, but scientists have shown that if you eat cooked foods with raw foods, and the raw foods form at least 50% of the meal, and you eat the raw foods before or with the cooked foods (not cooked first, then raw), then the immune response is negated. This is very useful to know when you are transitioning; that as long as you're eating more raw than cooked, you're basically on a raw food diet! You don't need to be 100% to get the benefits, and actually just 50-60% is a really good place to be.

It's a good idea to work with the seasons if you can. It's not essential, but you'll find it much easier if you work with nature's rhythms rather than against them. The best time to start on the programme is in the longer days of the year, ie between March and September. Unless you're very confident, or in urgent need of change, between October and February I would say you're better off waiting a little, doing some more research, stocking up on new foods and equipment, so you're ready to go when the seasons are. Also remember that new moon is the best time for starting new projects. A full moon is when we hold on, when we are not ready to let go. So if you start on a new moon, or at least in the first 14 days of the moon's cycle, you're going to get better results. Also the change of seasons is always a good time to begin a new programme, so within a week of either solstice or equinox. If you try the programme and don't get the results you were looking for, I'd say it's definitely worth trying again on a more auspicious date. The very best time to do anything like this is Spring Equinox, around the end of March.

Going raw is very much a transformational journey. You might already think of yourself as a happy, fulfilled and contented person, but once you start eating this way, you will discover all kinds of new ideas to squeeze more juice out of your life, new motivations and inspirations. It may help you to keep a journal, detailing how you're feeling every day. It's very common when a person starts detoxing for negative emotions to arise, so don't be afraid of looking at those. Allow them to pass, and don't attach to them. It's also common to experience more extreme highs and lows as your body and mind start to come into balance. Again, it may help to write things down. Sometimes I have an ongoing thought pattern in my head and when I actually put on paper it sounds so ridiculous I have to laugh at myself. By naming our fears, it helps lessen their power over us. I've included a whole chapter on the process of emotional detoxification, because I believe it's as key as the physical process.

Please read the menus through carefully before you start. You need to be able to fit in up to 60 mins of pre-prep time in the kitchen most days, so you have what you need ready for the following day. The pre-prep is mentioned at the end of the day before, so remember to check it in advance.

There are shopping lists attached which we have tried to make as accurate as possible, but please double check your requirements to match your own preferences eg if you're not keen on a certain food you need to decide what you're going to use as a substitute. If you spot any errors or omissions, please let us know.

Good luck! Don't forget, if you need more support and inspiration, check out **KateMagic.com**. And if you have any specific questions on the programme, please email **kate@rawliving.eu**. I am currently studying Functional Nutrition with Andrea Nakayama, and offer holistic health coaching in person or online, incorporating lifestyle, nutrition, mindfulness, yoga, meditation and reiki.

Dietary Trends

Trends become trends for a reason! There is always an element of sense to them, which is why they resonate with people and become popular. It's always a question of tailoring the diet to what is appropriate to you and your personal needs, and not being too dogmatic. Here are some notes, should you wish to adapt your menus to a specific set of dietary principles.

- **Intermittent Fasting.** The idea here is that when we have long periods of rest between meals, it gives the body plenty of time to rebuild and rejuvenate. I am a big fan of not eating late at night or early in the morning. If you can have your evening meal no later than 8pm, that's really going to benefit your digestion.
- **Keto.** To do a strict Keto diet, 80% of the calories in the diet should come from fat. You will notice that when we get into the fully raw days, we are heading in that direction. If Keto is something you are interested in, I think it works very well in combination with raw. My current feeling is that high carb works better for some people, and high fat works better for others, and that would be down to lifestyle as well as genetic predisposition. To do Raw Keto, you would need to use only stevia as a sweetener and eliminate fruits, and you would find yourself more or less there.
- **Paleo.** The thinking behind paleo is not to consume foods that haven't been eaten for over 2000 years. There is a lot of sense to this! Again, I feel Raw Paleo is something that can work very well, if that's what you are inclined towards, as the basis of the diet is fruit, vegetables, nuts and seeds.
- **Plant-based.** Some raw foodists do include raw dairy in their diets, and although this menu is fully vegan, I do feel small amounts of unpasteurised sheep's and goat's products can be helpful for some people. The majority raw foodists do not include raw meat, and although there is a small group who do (they call themselves Instinctos), I cannot recommend that.
- **Fodmaps.** A low Fodmaps diet is a low carbohydrate diet, and once again, the raw vegan diet lends itself easily to this adaptation. You would have to only include the low Fodmaps fruits such as bananas. The majority of vegetables are acceptable, although I have to say, I would struggle without broccoli, cauliflower or cabbage.

To my mind, the kind of raw vegan menu that we have covered this month combines the best principles of all these dietary interpretations. It's composed of traditional foods that for the most part our bodies should have no problems digesting. It's kind to the environment and the animals. When done with regard to sound nutritional principles, it's a high energy diet that promotes a healthy metabolism. If you have the enthusiasm, discipline and determination to stick with it, I truly believe there is no better way to eat. I hope this little book goes some way in supporting you in making the optimum choices for yourself on your own individual path to wholeness.

Breakfast

On rising, try and drink a minimum of one litre of liquids before you eat.

If you're making teas, they can be brewed and reheated throughout the day. I use a cafetiere for making tea: if you use a teapot you will find that bits get stuck in the spout, especially goji berries. Whichever teas you choose, all the quantities given in the recipes are for one litre of water.

Try not to boil your water! This might sound a little crazy at first, but get in the habit of making your tea with water heated to only 80 deg C, and you will notice the difference. Firstly, using boiling water destroys the flavour of the herbs, and secondly, it's too hot for the body to tolerate. I would recommend investing in a kettle with a temperature control; they are easy to find (I have a Cuisinart), but if you haven't got one, get in the habit of turning it off before it boils. 80 deg C is hot but not boiling; just about cool enough to drink straight away without burning.

Mid Morning

Drink a litre of your chosen beverage, if not more. Once you feel as if you've drunk as much as you can, and you're properly hungry, then it's time to eat. Ideally, this should be at least two hours after waking, although if it's sooner, don't worry, please go ahead and eat. The longer you can wait before eating solid food the better, as this gives your body more time to clean out from the day before. Don't wait until you're starving, just make sure you're actually physically hungry.

Try and eat until you're nearly full, not quite full. Eating until you're full at every meal is not advisable. The smaller portion sizes you consume, the more your body adjusts and soon you will be amazed at the small portions your body needs to feel satiated. This is all very nutrient dense food and you don't need to eat it in large quantities. The less you eat, the more your stomach shrinks, so you simply feel full quicker. There's a lot of studies that show that under-eating is one of the keys to longevity. Again, please do not take this as a cue to start starving yourself! Simply to be aware of the difference between how much you need to eat when you are feeding yourself with properly nutritious food, rather than how much you eat out of habit or because of emotional patterns.

If you need anything to keep you going between breakfast and lunch, drink some more before you reach for the snacks: tea, Mylk, juice, and coconut water are all good options.

Lunch

Lunch should happen 3-4 hours after breakfast. If you held out until 11.0 to eat breakfast, eat lunch at 2.0. If you had breakfast at 9.0, have lunch about 1.0. Please don't eat sooner than three hours or this will mess up your digestion. Please don't wait longer than five hours or you will get too hungry and when blood sugar drops, our minds get foggy and it's harder to make the best decisions and stay on track with our good intentions.

Mid Afternoon

Make your Mylk after lunch, and drink it during the afternoon. If you can't make it because you're not at home and don't have access to the right equipment, you can just make it in the morning and take it out with you. If you can keep it in the fridge it will be fine. If you can't keep it in the fridge, you probably want to have it between breakfast and lunch instead of lunch and dinner so it doesn't spoil.

At least two hours after lunch, enjoy a delicious treat. Even if you're not hungry! This will make you feel that you are spoiling yourself and indulging. It will take away feelings of denial or hardship. Eat as much of this treat as you feel like, you've done so well all day so far. If you eat double the amount of chocolate that you intended, it doesn't matter! It's all good for you. It is wonderful to be on this path, and you deserve the best.

If you habitually overeat when you don't want to, what you hopefully will find is that giving yourself permission to overeat on these amazingly healthy treats will remove the guilt and the lack of self-love around over-eating, because these foods are so full of nutrients and high vibrations that however much you eat you will still feel positive.

If you are not a habitual overeater, make sure to have a nibble anyway, just to check in with yourself and make sure you are feeling contented and satiated.

Dinner

Dinner should happen 2-3 hrs after your mid-afternoon snack, and about 5 hrs after your lunch. So if you had lunch at 12.0, a snack at 2.0, then you can eat dinner about 5.0. If lunch didn't happen until 2.0, and your snack at 4.0, eat dinner at 6.0 or 7.0. Please try not to eat this meal after 8.0pm. You should be all finished and cleared away by then! The earlier in the evening you eat this meal, the better you will feel when you wake up the next day.

If all this raw food is too much for you, now is the time to enjoy some cooked food with your dinner, especially in week one. If you want to eat cooked, choose steamed root vegetables, root vegetables baked in coconut oil, quinoa, or millet. Eat as much of these as you like to slow down the detox process if it's too much for you. Try and avoid meat, fish, wheat, dairy, grains, pulses. If you're seriously tempted by one of these foods, wait five days and see if it goes away. If the craving doesn't pass, eat and enjoy with a large green salad. Do not eat any processed foods with artificial additives and preservatives: make sure whatever you do, that your diet is 100% wholefoods.

Supper

If you are an early to bed person, you can skip this last meal. But if you're still hungry, a little snack before bedtime doesn't hurt. Pick something from the afternoon snack menu. Don't overeat though – if you feel the urge, hold back, and promise yourself a big breakfast tomorrow. You will wake up feeling a whole lot better. This meal should be very small, just a little snack. Some people like to eat it straight after dinner, as dessert. Others like to wait another few hours, until 9.0 or 10.0. If you are sensitive to chocolate, best not to eat it after 5.0pm, so make this meal something that doesn't involve superfoods.

It's important you get your green juice in at some point in the day. If you haven't had time to do it so far, enjoy it after dinner instead of a glass of wine. Making green juice only takes 10-15 mins, don't be scared of it! It makes all the difference in how you feel. These recipes given make approximately 500 ml; if you have the time, desire and budget, then I recommend doubling it and making a litre for optimum feelings of virtuousness.

If you had your green juice earlier in the day, have some more tea or a latte. You want to be drinking minimum three litres of liquids a day, but the more you can drink the better you will feel, and the easier the detox process. Contrary to popular understanding, plain water is not the most hydrating thing to drink. Plain water acts a flushing mechanism: drinks that contain minerals and healthy fats are more hydrating eg plant Mylks, juices, coconut water, kombucha.

I promise you, you won't go hungry on this programme! In fact, the reverse, you should feel like you are eating an abundance of food, and living like a King or a Queen!

A Note about Supplements

I believe that most of your nutritional requirements can be met adequately on a balanced raw vegan diet, but there are a few key areas that need to be addressed. I would highly recommend supplementing with an EPA/DHA supplement, to ensure you are getting enough of these essential fats. And a good quality mult-vit for vegans is also helpful – we use BetterYou and Garden of Life. The nutrients that you will almost definitely need to supplement with are Vitamins, D3, B12 & K2.

Day 1

Pre-prep (the day before):
Make raw chocolate
(See Page 88)
Make cereal (See Page 60)

In week one, we are going to be having a raw breakfast and snacks. Lunch and dinner will both be at least 50% raw, making your total raw intake for the week around 70%. This is to ease you into things gradually. As excited as you may be, you're going to get better results by taking it slowly. By the end of the month you'll be as raw as raw can be, and if you feel like it, you can stay there, so what's a few more weeks to lay a solid foundation?

Tea

Reishi & Goji Tea

1 tsp reishi extract, 1 tbsp goji berries, 1 litre hot water

Reishi substitutes: 1 tsp 3 immortals, 1 tsp cordyceps, 1 tsp chaga, 1 tsp 14 mushroom blend, 1 sachet Four Sigma Foods.

There are no substitutes for gojis! You would do well to buy 250g to last the month. If you really don't like them (or are averse to nightshades, they are part of the nightshade family), you could try Jujube dates in their place, or sweeten your tea with your sweetener of choice eg stevia, honey.

Breakfast

Cereal (See Page 60)

Makes eight portions. This will last you the whole of your first week. If you don't like cereal, skip onto the Day Nine breakfast. If you don't have time to make your own, you can buy one of the ready-made raw granolas on the market.

Lunch

Rice Cakes, Guacamole, Rocket & Crudités (See Page 62)

There's a Guacaomle recipe on p62. Homemade guac is a million times better than shop bought. Or if you're really in a hurry, just mash an avocado in a bowl with a fork! Heap the guac onto the rice cake and heap the rocket on top of that. Eat as many as you like. Punctuate with crudités dipped in the guac eg cauliflower, broccoli, pepper, carrot, cucumber.

Morning prep:
Soak almonds for Mylk

Mylk

Lucuma Blueberry Mylk
(See Page 56)

If you are in a hurry, or finding it difficult to drink that much liquid, you can start off by using half the amount of water ie 500 ml. This will make a thicker drink, more like a smoothie. Try and increase the amount of liquid you are using as the month goes by.

Snack

Raw Chocolate (See Page 88)

Of course, we have to introduce raw chocolate on day one of the programme. Try not to eat more than 40g in a day. There's a recipe for you attached. If you haven't got time to make it in advance you can stock up on your favourite raw chocolate bars instead.

Dinner

Green Salad & Baked Sweet Potato
(See Page 72)

Have one potato and fill up on salad. When enjoying raw foods and cooked foods together, the body benefits more if you don't eat the cooked foods first. So tuck into the salad first, and make sure you eat enough to feel satiated.

Green Juice

Green Juice Recipe One
(See Page 58)

Hands up who likes making juice? When I ask this in my classes, no-one ever says yes. That's why I don't have a juicer. But I do drink juice every day that I can. So how do I make it? With a blender and a Mylk bag. I chop all my veggies small, and blend them up in my blender to a pulp. We don't want to drink it like this though, because that's a lot of fibre to digest and not easy for our stomachs to handle. We want to remove all that fibre and leave the nutrient-rich juice that our cells can easily absorb. So we strain it through a Mylk bag (an essential piece of raw kitchen equipment), and not only have we made silky smooth juice in a very short time, we don't have to clean the juicer afterwards.

Affirmation

My physical form is a beautiful vessel for my soul to inhabit. I love the energy and vitality that it bestows on me.

Pre-prep for next day: Make chia cookies (dehydrator needed) (See Page 86)

Day 2

Tea
Ginger & Goji Tea

2 cm (1") fresh ginger root, finely diced, 1 tbsp goji berries, 1 litre hot water

Breakfast
Cereal (See Page 60)

Lunch
Oatcakes, Turmeric Butter, Alfalfa Sprouts & Cucumber (See Page 62)

Spread the oatcakes with the turmeric butter and heap with alfalfa sprouts. Eat as many as you like, alternating with the cucumber sticks, which you can also dip in the butter. Oats do not contain gluten.

Mylk
Purple Chia Mylk (See Page 56)

Snack
Chia Cookies (See Page 86)

Day two, and let's get straight in there with some cookies. If you don't have a dehydrator, then buy some of the pre-packaged raw cookies available – my favourites here in London are Cru8.

Dinner
Arame & Quinoa Salad (See Page 73)

Quinoa is actually technically a seed, which makes it much more digestible than some of the grains. Arame is a delicate Japanese seaweed which is an easy one to start with. This is a really nutritious and filling but quick to make dinner; eat as much as you want and then follow it up with some raw chocolate if you need a little dessert.

Green Juice
Green Juice Recipe Two (See Page 58)

Affirmation
All my trillions of cells are filled with love and light. I release everything that no longer serves me, so I am simply pure love and light.

Morning prep: Soak arame for lunch and chia for making cookies

Day 3

Week 1

Tea

Eterniteea

This is my Reishi tea blend. If you prefer not to use it, you can replace with your own favourite herbal tea. Loose leaf tea is much more beneficial than tea bags; the only company I know of who use medicinal grade herbs in their teas are Pukka.

You want to drink at least a litre of tea. You can usually get a few brews out of loose leaf tea, so don't throw the herbs away after the first brew, rebrew later in the day, or it's fine to leave them in the cafetiere and use them again the next day.

Breakfast

Cereal (See Page 60)

Lunch

Nori Rolls

You might already find yourself with leftovers of salad, guac, crudités, or quinoa. This is the best use for nori rolls! Take your nori sheets and layer them with whatever tempts you from the fridge. You can include sprouts, sauerkraut, some wasabi or mustard if you have it. Eat as many as you like; I am happy with just one, but you might find two is what you crave to feel satiated.

Mylk

Baobab Hemp Mylk (See Page 56)

Snack

Trail Mix (See Page 86)

Make your own trail mix from a combination of the following: goji berries, golden berries, raisins, coconut flakes, shelled hemp seeds, bee pollen, cacao nibs. Or buy some ready made trail mix such as Magic Mix. Eat as much as you like.

Dinner

Millet & Spinach Salad (See Page 73)

Quinoa and millet are the top two cooked foods I would recommend eating, as well as cooked vegetables. Millet is so economical and easy to make, and so sustaining. Make more than you need and have the rest for lunch tomorrow, cold.

Green Juice

Green Juice Recipe Three (See Page 58)

Affirmation

The universe loves me and it wants me to be happy.

Day 4

Tea

Infiniteea

This is my ashwagandha tea blend. As previously, if you have a preference for a different herbal tea, substitute that instead, but look for loose leaf teas with medicinal properties to set you up for the day.

Breakfast

Cereal (See Page 60)

Lunch

Millet & Spinach Salad (See Page 73)

Yesterday's leftovers. Add some extra green leaf eg lettuce, rocket, or baby leaf spinach, so it's half greens, half millet, and less dense than the dinner you had last night.

Mylk

Flax Maca Mylk (See Page 57)

Snack

Raw Chocolate (See Page 88)

Try not to eat more than 40g!

Dinner

Tempeh Stir Fry (See Page 74)

Tempeh is a fermented soy product, making it easier to digest than regular soy. It has a wonderful meaty flavour and texture, and with the current rise in veganism, is much more widely available than it used to be. It's perfect in a stir fry, but if you love it, you can also cube it and throw it into your salads in the coming days, it doesn't necessarily need cooking. Stir fry is a quick and easy dish that means you can cook your veggies for just enough time to soften them and bring out the flavours, but not too long to start losing their nutritional value. A great fall-back option when raw is not cutting it for you.

Green Juice

Green juice Recipe Four
(See Page 58)

Affirmation

Miracles are what the universe is made of, they show up in my life in both little ways and big ways every single day.

Morning prep:
Soak flax

Day 5  Week 1

Morning prep:
Soak hemp for Mylk

Tea
Lemon Ginger & Goji Tea

Take half small lemon or quarter large lemon and cut it into chunks. Put it in the pot with 2cm (1 inch) fresh ginger root, finely sliced, and 1 tbsp goji berries.

Breakfast
Cereal (See Page 60)

Lunch
Hummus, Corn Chips & Crudités
(See Page 64)

There's a hummus recipe included for you, but you can just buy some if you don't have the extra time or energy. Make your crudités from your favourite raw vegetables eg cauliflower, broccoli, pepper, cucumber, carrot, celery. Make sure you're eating at least as many veggie sticks as corn chips!

Mylk
Vanilla Hemp Mylk (See Page 57)

Snack
Chia Cookies (See Page 86)

Dinner
Tahini Kale Salad & Roasted Veggies (See Page 74)

This is the ultimate comfort food in my opinion! You can't fail to feel at peace with yourself and the world with a belly full of kale and root veg. And the advantage of eating such a high fibre meal is that you're going to feel full in your stomach long before you're at risk of consuming too many calories.

Green Juice
Green Juice Recipe Five (See Page 58)

Affirmation
I am grateful for the adventure of having a body. I am especially grateful for my organs of digestion which work so hard every day: my mouth, oesophagus, liver, gall bladder kidneys, stomach and gut!

Evening pre-prep:
Make bread
(See Page 75)

Day 6

Tea

Gynostemma Ginger & Goji Tea

Gynostemma is my favourite herb for tea making. If you prefer not to use it, substitute with your own favourite herbal tea, but please ensure to use loose dried herbs. Or a good shortcut is to use the Dragon Herbs Spring Dragon teabags. Gynostemma expands a lot in water, you need much less than you think, just 1 tbsp or a small handful. Put in the pot with 2cm (1") fresh ginger root, finely sliced, and 1 tbsp goji berries.

Breakfast

Cereal (See Page 60)

Lunch

Stuffed Avocado (See Page 63)

Supplement with rice cakes or oat cakes if still hungry.

Mylk

Chocolate Hemp Mylk (See Page 56)

Snack

Trail Mix (See Page 86)

Dinner

Reuben's Tomato Soup & Authentic Bread (See Page 75)

Make your bread in advance the night before (page 75) - if you time it right, you can eat it warm, straight out of the dehydrator. If you haven't got time, a loaf of your favourite kind of bread will do just fine, you're still in transition week.

Reuben is my eldest son who helped with the proof-reading of this book, so I had to include one of his recipes as a little shout out to him. He is an amazing chef; he used to make this recipe all the time when he was a teenager, it was his favourite dinner.

Green Juice

Green Juice Recipe Six (See Page 59)

Affirmation

Right now, everything is exactly how it should be, and everything is working out perfectly for me.

Pre-prep:
Make candy for tomorrow's snack (See Page 88)
Kale chips (See Page 64)

Day 7

Morning prep:
Make kale chips if you are not buying ready-made ones
Soak hazelnuts for Mylk

Tea

Schizandra & Goji Tea

1 tbsp schizandra berries and 1 tbsp goji berries

Schizandra means "five-flavour berry." It is considered a superior herb in Chinese medicine and is extremely rebalancing. It has a peculiar flavour which I love: sweet and bitter all at the same time. You can use dried schizandra berries, or we also have schizandra eeTea from Dragon Herbs which makes it even easier.

Breakfast

Cereal (See Page 60)

Lunch

Kale Chips & Tomato Salad
(See Page 64)

Kale Chips are the bomb! Just writing about them makes me want to go and make a batch. If you can buy some pre-made ones, that's a viable option, but making your own is an infinitely better bet. If you don't have a dehydrator, you can bake them instead, they are just as tasty.

The tomato salad is all about the quality of tomatoes you buy. You might go for little baby cherry tomatoes or big fat beefsteaks. I love purple tomatoes, and if you purchased a combination of purple, yellow and red, you could make the most beautiful tomato salad your kitchen had ever seen.

Mylk

Hazelnut Cardamom Mylk
(See Page 57)

Snack

Candy (See Page 88)

Dinner

Your favourite dinner?

It's your first week completed! Well done. How are you feeling? Treat yourself to your favourite meal. Try and avoid meat, dairy and wheat - make it vegan and gluten-free if you possibly can. Observe how it tastes, and how it feels in the body afterwards. Make some notes if you're keeping a food journal: how did you feel buying or preparing it, were you more excited than usual or did you have mixed feelings? How did it taste, better than usual, or not the same? How did you feel afterwards? There are no right or wrong answers, the important part is the observation process so that you begin tuning into your body and your consciousness on a deeper level, and really pay attention to working out what serves you best. Follow it with a raw dessert or raw chocolate if you like.

Green Juice

Green Juice Recipe Seven
(See Page 59)

Affirmation

I am able to handle today's challenges calmly and capably, and I am proud of my ability to deal with tricky situations and maintain my inner peace, or at least regain it very quickly!

Pre-prep:
Blueberry Pie
(See Page 87)

Crudités

Day 8

Week 2

In week two, we are going to omit the cooked food at lunchtime, and just have up to 50% raw at dinner. This makes our total raw intake for the week at around 80%.

The teas, juices and Mylks are repeated from the first week. If you had a favourite, have it more often, and if there was one you didn't like, skip it. They are all interchangeable.

Tea
Reishi & Goji Tea

Breakfast
Cereal (See Page 60)

Lunch
What was your favourite lunch from last week? Repeat that.

When we eat optimum foods, we often find ourselves craving the same thing day after day. This happens when the body detects some vital nutrients in a certain food and excitedly asks us if we can stock up! In a modern day diet, the quest for an endless variety of foods is more about a bored palate than anything else. Any parent will tell you how kids are happy to eat the same food every day for weeks on end; this is because the body prefers to work with simple messages.

Hopefully there was something you ate in this past week that really hit the spot and had you craving more. So joyfully revisit that dish and eat it frequently until the craving diminishes.

Mylk

Snack
Blueberry Pie (See Page 87)

Dinner
What was your favourite dinner from last week? Repeat that.

Green Juice

Affirmation
I love spending money on things I really want, and spreading wealth around. I love how abundant the world is, and how rich my life experience feels.

Evening prep: Make chia porridge (See Page 60)

Day 9

Tea
Ginger & Goji Tea

Breakfast
Chia Porridge (See Page 60)

The quantities given make enough for four portions, so I recommend having it for the next four days. It will keep fine in the fridge for this length of time, and that way you don't have to worry about making breakfast every day.

Lunch
Nori Rolls (See Page 19)

We had these in week one, but this time we are doing them fully raw. Nori rolls are one of my staple lunches that I enjoy over and over again by changing up the basic ingredients. Use something creamy eg avocado or some leftover dip, something spicy eg wasabi paste or mustard, and fill with crudités, green leaves, and beansprouts. Eat as many as you like.

Mylk

Snack
Raw Chocolate (See Page 88)

Dinner
Honey Roasted Parsnips and Rocket Salad (See Page 76)

Vegans can omit the honey! Use coconut nectar or maple syrup instead to bring out the natural sweetness of the parsnips.

Green Juice

Affirmation
I am loved. Everyone I meet treats me kindly, respectfully and considerately.

Pre-prep:
Make chia crackers
(See Page 65)

Day  10

Tea
Eterniteea

Breakfast
Chia Porridge (See Page 60)

Lunch
Turmeric Butter & Crackers
(See Page 62/65)

Spread your dip on the crackers and heap as big a pile as you can of your favourite greens on top eg rocket, spinach, alfalfa. Eat as many as you like, I'm quite happy with two, but on hungry days I need three.

Mylk

Snack
Candy (See Page 88)

Dinner
Pasta in a Raw Marinara
(See Page 76)

I would recommend using spelt, corn or rice pasta. While it's cooking, make your raw sauce in the blender (recipe attached). No need to warm the sauce, when you pour it over the pasta it will heat gently. Eat immediately.

Green Juice

Affirmation
I love eating such wonderful healthy foods and I am proud of how well I look after my body.

Day 11

Tea
Infiniteea

Breakfast
Chia Porridge (See Page 60)

Lunch
Guacamole Wraps (See Page 62)

Make your favourite guacamole recipe, or use the one given. Take romaine lettuce leaves and scoop the guacamole into the centre of the leaf. Add some beansprouts or alfalfa sprouts, and roll the leaf over to make a wrap. Eat as many as you like.

Mylk

Snack
Trail Mix (See Page 86)

Dinner
Spinach & Potato Curry (See Page 77)

Like when we made the pasta yesterday, the hot potatoes will warm the raw curry sauce, so you might even not guess it wasn't a completely cooked meal. Sag Aloo, to give it its proper Indian name, was one of my favourite transitional meals.

Green Juice

Affirmation
I am in the perfect position to achieve all the things I want to achieve, today and every day. I know that there is always more to dream and more to do, so I enjoy the process of ever-expansion, and don't pressure or put stress on myself.

Pre-prep:
Make a second batch of chia porridge. Change up the fruits and nuts or seeds that you add to it.

Pre-prep for tomorrow's lunch:
Raw hummus (See Page 64)

Day 12

Tea
Lemon Ginger & Goji

Breakfast
Chia Porridge (See Page 60)

Lunch
Raw Hummus, Crudités & Olives
(See Page 64)

Serve hummus with crudités, and olives, plus a few crackers if you need something more filling. Eat as much of this hummus with veggie sticks as you like, it's all good.

Mylk

Snack
Blueberry Pie (See Page 87)

Dinner
Steamed Broccoli & Coleslaw
(See Page 77)

There is never a bad time to eat broccoli. And this coleslaw is a staple recipe you can always come back to. I like to use purple carrots, or you could also sub beetroot for the cabbage in order to jazz it up.

Green Juice

Affirmation
Everything is always working out for me. Sometimes I can't see how, but that doesn't mean that I don't trust that it is.

Pre-prep:
Make Bayonnaise
for tomorrow's lunch
(See Page 65)

Day 13

Tea
Gynostemma Ginger & Goji

Breakfast
Chia Porridge (See Page 60)

Lunch
Bayonnaise & Crackers
(See Pages 65)

Spread the crackers with Bayonnaise, as thick as you like. I love the contrast of the smooth creamy dip with the crunchy crackers. Top with alfalfa, spinach, or lettuce, whichever is your favourite, maybe some avocado slices as well. Eat as many as you like.

Mylk

Snack
Candy (See Page 88)

Dinner
Thai Yellow Curry (See Page 78)

This is one of my most popular recipes. You can warm it gently to bring out the flavours and make it more satisfying. Serve with rice noodles if you want it to be more filling.

Green Juice

Affirmation

I embrace challenges as ways to prove to myself how well I respond and how quickly I can find solutions. I am good at overcoming my fears and working through my self-limiting belief systems in order to realise what an all-powerful being I truly am.

Pre-prep:
Make pumpkin pâté
(Page 66)

Day 14

Tea
Schizandra & Goji Tea

Breakfast
Chia Porridge (See Page 60)

Lunch
Pumpkin Seed Wraps

This combination of pumpkin seeds and sun-dried tomatoes is such a flavour bomb. Basically, you can do anything you like with it, but today I recommend wrapping it in lettuce leaves and enjoying your fill of wraps.

Mylk

Snack
Raw Chocolate (See Page 88)

Dinner
It's a free dinner night again! What are you going to have this time?

The same as last week or is there something else you've been missing? Again, observe its effects in the body, and compare them to last week. Please definitely avoid meat, dairy and gluten at this point because eating any of those food groups could really set you back.

This will be your last cooked meal for two weeks, enjoy it! The emotions we invest into a meal affect us almost as much as the nutrients a food contains. Whatever your choices, be sure to eat your food with appreciation. If you're keeping a food journal, record how you experience this meal compared to the cheat night you had a week ago. It will also be interesting to compare how this meal works for you when you enjoy it again after the month is up.

Green Juice

Affirmation
I am kind and loving towards myself, I don't over-analyse, judge or criticise when I feel like I might have done things differently. I accept that we all make mistakes, and as long as I am learning and growing, the best thing to do is to pick myself up and carry on.

Pre-prep: Make Shortbread (See Page 86)

Kale Caesar Salad

Day 15

Week 3

It's week three and we are diving into fully raw! I won't say 100% because we are still using some superfoods and seasonings that aren't raw, but it's as good as. This is pretty much how I eat, although generally in smaller quantities. You should really be starting to feel a difference in energy levels now: a new-found levity about life that you had been missing previously. Keep going, meal by meal, and remember, the most important part of your transition is learning to pay attention to the process of how the food affects your physical, mental and emotional energy systems, so you get really plugged into that inner guidance system of yours.

Tea

You should have tried each of the tea suggestions twice by now. There were lots of different variations on each of the seven recipes, maybe you want to revisit them and vary them slightly. Maybe there was one that you particularly enjoyed that you want to have repeatedly. Or perhaps you've been inspired to create your own medicinal tea blend! The choice is yours. Just make sure you drink at least a litre a day of these teas. As your body is starting to cleanse, you might find that you can easily manage two litres a day, that would be wonderful. I usually don't have any problem drinking two litres during the course of a morning. This helps cleanse me out before I start putting any solid food in.

Breakfast

Chia Porridge (See Page 60)

Lunch

Repeat your favourite

Mylk

Snack

Shortbread (See Page 86)

Dinner

Stuffed Avocado & Spinach Salad (See Page 78)

A side salad, as you've hopefully picked up now, is mainly a question of finding good quality green leaves and piling them up on your plate with an exciting dressing. As far as spinach goes, I prefer baby leaf spinach because it's less bitter, has more flavour, and is lower in oxalic acid. This tahini-maca dressing is a winner; the original recipe can be found in the Raw Magic book, and is one of Boy George's favourites!

Green Juice

Affirmation

I am safe and protected. Angels are guiding me, and keeping negative energies at bay.

Pre-prep:
Pre-prep pizza
(See Page 79)

Day 16

Week 3

Tea

Breakfast
Chia Porridge (See Page 60)

Lunch
Hemp Tabbouleh (See Page 66)

We are going to make double quantities of this and save some for tomorrow. It's a good habit to get into with your raw food prep to make more than you need at one meal and serve it in a different way the next day. This means you're not in the kitchen forever, and as most raw food dishes actually taste better the next day, once the flavours have had a chance to marinade, you're improving the deliciousness of your meals as well.

Mylk

Snack
Blueberry Pie (See Page 87)

Dinner
Instant Pizza (see Page 79)

There are so many ways to do raw pizza, it's really up to you whether you want to make it super simple, or spend the day in the kitchen playing. At it's most basic, it's just crackers spread with tomato sauce and topped with a little diced veg. I've given you a simple recipe, but feel free to expand on it any way you choose. If you have time to pop it in the dehydrator for a few hours, that adds a whole new layer of flavour sensation. Currently, my favourite home-made pizzas are the ones I make using the Wrawp pizza bases, that I assemble and then pop in the dehydrator for an hour to meld the layers.

Green Juice

Affirmation
I am getting what I want out of life, I understand where I am in the bigger picture of things and have a clear sense of how I am moving in directions that are exciting to me.

Pre-prep:
Make Falafel for tomorrow's dinner (See Page 79)
Soak oats overnight

Day 17

Tea

Breakfast
Oats (See Page 60)
Use about 100g (1 cup) per serving

Lunch
Sunshine Soup (See Page 68)

Mylk

Snack
Chia Cookies (See Page 86)

Dinner
Falafel & Hemp Tabbouleh
(See Page 79/66)

We are using yesterday's tabbouleh, and the falafel we made last night. You might still have some hummus or guac left that you can also include in the meal. This is a great example of a gourmet meal that takes no time at all to serve, as you've already done all the prep work in advance.

Green Juice

Affirmation
Every cell of my being is filled with love and light and that, radiates out of me to uplift everyone I meet, whether they know it or not. This energy transference is a way to help people when maybe words and deeds can't reach them, so I am never powerless.

Pre-prep:
Soak oats overnight

Day 18

Tea

Breakfast

Oats (See Page 60)

Use about 100g (1 cup) per serving

Lunch

Sushi (See Page 83)

This cauliflower rice is one of my favourites, I make it all the time. Use some in your nori today and then save the rest for your curry in a few days (it will keep fine). Put your rice in the nori along with slices of avocado, pickled ginger, rocket, pickled cucumber, wasabi or whatever else you favour.

Mylk

Snack

Candy (See Page 88)

Dinner

Courgette Noodles in Marinara Sauce (See Page 76)

A spiralizer is such a handy piece of kitchen equipment, I have a small manual one, like a pencil sharpener, that does the job really well and doesn't take up any space in the kitchen. I also take it with me when I'm travelling.

If you don't have a spiralizer, you can use a mandolin, or at a push a potato peeler, to create ribbons from your courgette.

You might have leftover marinara from the pizza two nights ago, in which case you can whip this one up in minutes.

Green Juice

Affirmation

I am a magnet for prosperity and abundance, I manifest everything I need easily and effortlessly, in a way that can feel surprising, but wonderful. This prosperity is my natural state, no matter what my childhood programming might be telling me.

Pre-prep:
Tacos for dinner tomorrow (See Page 82)
Soak oats overnight

Day 19

Tea

Breakfast

Oats (See Page 60)

Use about 100g (1 cup) per serving

Lunch

Cucumber Salad & Cauliflower Cheese (See Page 68)

Another gourmet lunch you can rustle up in no time. Never underestimate the humble cucumber! With the right dressings, it's a scene stealer all by itself. To switch it up a little, you can try spiralising the cucumber. The cauliflower cheese is great dehydrated, if you have time, just 4hrs is enough to warm it through and soften the cauliflower a little, or put it on the night previous, before you go to bed, and it goes really crispy and crunchy.

Mylk

Snack

Trail Mix (See Page 86)

Dinner

Nori Tacos (See Page 82)

Tacos coming from Mexico, and California being heavily influenced by Mexican cuisine, and raw foods being led by California, tacos are pretty much a staple raw food item. You can add some guac or "cheese" (the Turmeric Butter) recipe, if you have them left. You can also use the same base constituent ingredients to create Nachos and Enchiladas.

Green Juice

Affirmation

I have so much to be grateful for, the world is a beautiful place, there are so many blessings around me when I open my eyes and choose to see them.

Pre-prep:
Soak oats overnight

Day 20

Week 3

Tea

Breakfast

Oats (See Page 60)

Use about 100g (1 cup) per serving

Lunch

Mediterranean Salad

(See Page 69)

Mylk

Snack

Shortbread (See Page 86)

Dinner

Umami Kale & Kelp Noodles

(See Page 80)

This is one of my favourite recipes! I love kale and kelp noodles together. I also do kelp noodles and sauerkraut together a lot. And the pumpkin seed butter dressing is next level. I can make this dish in no time and it tastes better than anything you get in a restaurant..

Green Juice

Affirmation

I am nourished on all levels: not just through my food choices, but through the people I interact with and my life experiences.

Pre-prep:
Cake or dessert. Browse some raw recipe books or online resources and see what takes your fancy. Soak oats overnight

Day 21

Tea

Breakfast

Oats (See Page 60)
Use about 100g (1 cup) per serving

Lunch

Sauerkraut Slaw (See Page 69)

Mylk

Snack

Raw Chocolate (See Page 88)

Dinner

Cauliflower Rice & Curry
(See Page 83)

You're using the leftover cauliflower rice from Day 18, so you've just got to make the curry. The rice actually tastes better when it is a few days old and the flavours have had a chance to marinade and mingle.

Your favourite raw dessert

No favourite dinner night this week, sorry. But it's still pig-out time! And if you've got a sweet tooth, you might like this one even better. Choose your favourite raw dessert or cake, and eat as much of it as you would like. Once more, observe the process. How does it feel to pig-out on healthy food compared to unhealthy food? What emotions and patterns are coming up for you? How do you feel afterwards and the next day? It's important that you are aware of your relationship to food rather than using the diet as a way of limiting yourself. If you don't examine your weaknesses and vulnerabilities from the beginning, you're just storing them up to hit you harder later on. From now on, at least once a week, check in with yourself like this, indulge your cravings, and compassionately observe the physical and emotional processes of transformation.

Green Juice

Affirmation

When I need assistance, it comes speedily and easily, I receive all the help I need.

Pre-prep:
Soak oats overnight
Crackers & Chocolate Spread
(See Page 61)
The crackers need to go into the dehydrator so they are ready for breakfast not tomorrow, but the day after. Chocolate spread doesn't take long to make and is well worth the effort.

Day 22

Week 4

Week Four and you're nearly home. Just keep it at the same level as last week and you're doing great. At this stage, you've done most of the hard work, you've just got to sustain it. Don't give up now! You'll feel incredible once you've completed the month.

Tea

Breakfast

Oats (See Page 60)

Use about 100g (1 cup) per serving

Lunch

Repeat your favourite lunch from the menu so far

Mylk

Snack

Chia Cookies (See Page 86)

Dinner

Repeat your favourite dinner from the menu so far

Another fun thing about raw food prep is that because you're working with fresh ingredients, no two dishes ever taste the same. Guaranteed, the dish you're going to make tonight won't come out the same as last time. It's another way that means raw foods never gets boring.

Green Juice

Affirmation

I am a compassionate being in a compassionate universe. I understand everyone is on their own unique journey with their own individual struggles, and people extend the same respect to me in return.

Pre-prep:
Soak walnuts for Muhammara (See Page 69)
Soak oats overnight

Day 23

Tea

Breakfast
Crackers & Chocolate Spread (See Page 61)

Lunch
Muhammara (See Page 69)

Muhammara is a traditional Middle Eastern dip, a bit like hummus, which is so easy to do raw. Its basic ingredients are red peppers and walnuts, which when blended together make a pungent dip with all the versatility of hummus. I've left it open for you what to do with it: you can use it as the filling in a wrap with lettuce leaves or nori sheets, or now would be a good time to try the coconut wraps we stock on Raw Living, just made from young coconut meat. You might want to spread it on crackers or bread, or just have it alongside a salad

Mylk

Snack
Blueberry Pie (See Page 87)

Dinner
Beet It Soup (See Page 82)

This soup is best served lightly warmed. To warm foods through, use a heat-proof bowl stood in a pan of lightly simmering water, a Porringer (a double saucepan you can buy from Raw Living) or a Thermomix (the Rolls Royce of kitchen equipment!). Serve with bread or crackers (preferably raw ones!).

Green Juice

Affirmation
I am so creative and productive! It feels good to get so much done, and I complete my tasks effortlessly and joyously

Day 24

Tea

Breakfast
Crackers & Chocolate Spread (See Page 61)

Lunch
Sandwiches

Use your flax crackers from Day 10, or whatever crackers you have bought. Spread with leftover Bayonnaise, hummus, or pumpkin pâté . Heap up a cracker with tomato slices, pickled cucumber, alfalfa, rocket, whatever your favourites are, and then sandwich another cracker on top. Eat as many as you like.

Mylk

Snack
Shortbread (See Page 86)

Dinner
Kale Caesar Salad (See Page 84)

I often serve this salad at dinner parties and retreats, it's always a big hit. The capers and sun-dried tomatoes really pop against the heartiness of kale, and the creamy dill dressing is a winner all by itself, that can be used as a dip or a spread. This one keeps well, so it's a good one to make a big batch of and then eat it when it's a day or two old, and the kale has really started to soften and the flavours marinade.

Green Juice

Affirmation
Those closest to me show me unconditional love and support, and I am grateful for the ways in which they do that.

Day 25

Tea

Breakfast
Crackers & Chocolate Spread (See Page 61)

Lunch
Kimchi Salad (See Page 70)

Kimchi is one of my favourite foods, a Korean fermented vegetable which is made specially tasty with the inclusion of gochugaru, or Korean chilli flakes. If you're buying authentic Kimchi, and you're a vegetarian, check that it doesn't contain fish sauce, the traditional recipe often does. Many health food stores sell vegan brands now, and we have some on Raw Living.

Mylk

Snack
Candy (See Page 82)

Dinner
Sea Spaghetti in a Sour Cream or Pesto Sauce (See Page 84)

Sea spaghetti is a very popular sea vegetable that we use as a pasta replacement. It is incredibly dense nutritionally and very satisfying to eat. You can use your leftover sour cream from the Tacos as a dressing, or I've given you a pesto recipe. You could also use the Marinara recipe we used before with the Courgette Noodles..

Green Juice

Affirmation
I have all the time I need to get everything done, I am not rushed, I move at the ideal speed for me through my life.

Pre-prep: Make stuffed peppers (See Page 85)

Day

Week 4

Tea

Breakfast
Crackers & Chocolate Spread (See Page 61)

Lunch
Carrot & Spinach Soup (See Page 70)

Mylk

Snack
Trail Mix (See Page 86)

Dinner
Sunflower Stuffed Peppers (See Page 85)

Green Juice

Affirmation
I love my liver. I really love my liver so much. I am grateful for this complex and hard-working organ that supports my body with the burden of detoxification.

Stuffed Peppers

Day 27

Tea

Breakfast
Crackers & Chocolate Spread
(See Page 61)

Lunch
Wrawps

I love Wrawps! My favourites are the spirulina. They transform any meal into a feast. Stuff them with all your favourite salad ingredients. Or if you prefer, you can make your own wraps in the dehydrator. We also sell Pure Wraps, made with coconut, or Raw Wraps, made with spinach or kale, which are really good too.

Mylk

Snack
Raw Chocolate (See Page 88)

Dinner
Instant Kelp Noodles (See Page 85)

I love to eat kelp noodles once a week, I've yet to tire of them after being introduced to them over 12 years ago. Just seaweed and water, they meet every dietary requirement and are endlessly versatile. This is an easy quick recipe which doesn't even require the blender.

Green Juice

Affirmation
I am always amply rewarded for everything I do and all the energy I put in. I allow the universe's abundance to touch me in all kinds of unexpected and surprising ways.

Pre-prep: Prepare for the feast (See Page 47)

Day

Tea

Breakfast
Crackers & Chocolate Spread
(See Page 61)

Lunch
Ramen (See Page 71)

Last lunch and one of the best examples of how easy and delicious raw foods can be! A spiralizer is such a handy piece of equipment, I highly recommend you invest in one. However, if you don't have a spiralizer, you can use a mandolin, or at a push a potato peeler to create ribbons from your courgette. Pesto is super easy, it's all about the quality of your basil, get it good and fresh!

Mylk

Snack
Blueberry Pie (See Page 87)

Dinner
Have a feast!

Invite three of your raw curious friends round and make them your favourite dishes from the month - a drink, a lunch as a starter, a dinner as a main, and a dessert, with raw chocolate and your favourite tea to follow. Or better still, ask them to bring a raw dish each (so you don't have to do all the work) and have a potluck! Talk to them honestly about the week, the ups and the downs, and your intentions for your diet in the future. Ask them if they want to start a potluck group, where you all meet once a month and share raw dishes together. Potlucks are a very popular and easy way to keep you inspired about raw, as you know you have something to look forward to every month, and a place to share with like-minded individuals. You could maybe watch a raw-related film (see list on page 95) to get you inspired.

Green Juice

Affirmation
I am a beautiful person. Everyone loves me.

Now you've finished, hopefully you feel like you could carry on forever. Well, you can! Remember that if you have cravings acknowledge them, indulge them with compassion, and observe the processes. If fully raw isn't working for you for whatever reasons, be they physical or emotional or just practical, go back to the week one diet, and try and maintain at least 50% raw, while avoiding grains, dairy and animal products as much as you can. You should have a feeling now for what's realistic for you to maintain, what your favourites are, and what you thrive on. It's completely normal to have up and down phases like this in the beginning. Keep in mind that it's a long-term process that takes years to perfect and do your best to eat what makes you happiest. When eating less than optimum foods, try to ensure they are of the highest quality: organic wholegrains, not refined white grains, organic dairy and meat products, not products from factory farming that have been pumped full of hormones and steroids.

Transitional Support

Self-care

Health is as much about lifestyle as it is the food that you eat. Just changing your diet won't affect real transformation. It's essential for the success of this programme that you ensure you make time for self-care during this month as well. Self-care is highly individual, and only you can know what that looks like for you. Here are some suggestions of popular ways in which we can take time out for ourselves to effectively recharge and nurture our energies.

Ecotherapy - Spending time in nature is the number one failsafe cure-all. The power of just 20 mins brisk walking in nature can never be underestimated for calming the mind, and bringing us back into our bodies. Sunshine is important in the production of vitamin D in the body, which amongst other things is a precursor to dopamine, the hormone associated with drive and desire. Not spending enough time outdoors leads to a lack of motivation and a feeling of apathy.

Hydrotherapy - Water is an essential element for life, so spending time in and around water is compulsory. Swim, go take a spa day, run an aromatherapy bath.

Pampering - Do a face mask, get a massage, paint your nails (I am not a fan of nail salons where the technicians are exposing themselves to toxic chemicals all day for low wages, instead invest in a natural brand and do it yourself or with a girlfriend).

Culture - Go out and enjoy culture in communion with others: to the movies, live music, theatre, art exhibitions.

Movement - Take the stairs not the elevator, walk or cycle over public transport, stand in preference to sitting. Sedentary lifestyles are unnatural and depressing. Keep moving throughout your day in whichever ways that presents itself. See how far you can get through the day without sitting down: it gets easier with practice. Enjoy sports or yoga at least three times a week.

Sleep Hygiene - Be protective about your bedtime schedule: I believe sleeping at regular hours is more important than the amount of sleep we get. Sleep with blackout blinds or an eye mask to allow the pineal gland to produce sufficient melatonin. Make your bedroom a sanctuary of crystals, plants and pillows; sleep with no electrics in the bedroom, especially WiFi, to allow your electromagnetic field to recharge.

Sweat - Support your detoxification process. Your liver is working so hard, it will really appreciate all the assistance you give it. Sweating it out in a steam-room or sauna, preferably an infra-red sauna, is one of the best ways to remove the burden of toxicity from your cells. In addition, on a raw food diet, it's essential we sweat regularly to avoid stagnation in the body.

Enemas and Colonics - I am big into enemas and colonics as a way of supporting your body in removing what it is releasing (if you put "Kate Magic enemas" into YouTube, you will find my enema video, which is my most popular YouTube video and probably not for the right reasons). Colonics are more efficient, if your budget can stretch to them; enemas will do just fine if not, and are easier because you administer them yourself in the privacy of your own home. If you don't find them too challenging, try keeping them up and doing one at least every two weeks during the transition period, this will really help your progress. They keep you feeling clear and positive, and help you to not get stuck in old patterns. I recommend an enema or colonic during the first week, and a second one at the end of the fourth week.

Meditate - Meditation is one of the easiest and most overlooked ways to improve your health. Start with 8 minutes a day. Think of it etting all these thoughts out on paper. You will see some of the things you get preoccupied with are a bit silly and don't really matter in the bigger scheme of things, while others are important for you to take a proper look at, and need further attention. Plus, it makes a fascinating artefact to look back on, and remind you where it all started! Just a year down the line, we can be taking for granted the things that we worked so hard to achieve, so it's wonderful to have a reminder of how far we have come.

Mindfulness - Cultivate awareness of your inner dialogue, and don't be harsh on yourself if you deviate from your good intentions. For more advice on magical thinking, see the section at the end of the book. How we talk to ourselves is perhaps the most key component in everything we do. Gratitude, acceptance, and self-love make everything more harmonious, and lighter. It's not supposed to be hard! Assume life is always working out for you (because it is), and make ease and openness your default setting.

Community - Feeling supported on our journey is one of the key components of success. If you don't have anyone in your life who is cheering you on in your health journey, make it your mission to find them. Starting potluck groups in your area is very often successful: you might be surprised to find the amount of others who are on a similar path to you, and sharing that commonality of experience is so motivating. If you already have supportive friends or family, involve them in your end of week feasts and let them know how much you value their being there for you.

Journalling - Keeping a journal can be really helpful in observing your relationship with food as you transition. In Functional Nutrition, we ask our clients to keep a "Food Mood Poop" Journal, monitoring what they ate, how they felt, and how their elimination was daily, in order to investigate what foods work and what foods don't. You can also journal all the emotions around food that come up for you, both positive and negative. This could be things like, "Today I was craving curry and nan bread because that was a treat for us as a family when I was a kid," or "Today I noticed how awful the meat section of the supermarket smelt, I never noticed it before." "Today I felt really good because I didn't overeat in the evenings like I usually do", or "I woke up feeling not hungry at all which isn't like me." Journalling like this is invaluable in clearing your mind by getting all these thoughts out on paper. You will see some of the things you get preoccupied with are a bit silly and don't really matter in the bigger scheme of things; while others are important for you to take a proper look at, and need further attention. Plus, it makes a fascinating artefact to look back on, and remind you where it all started! Just a year down the line, we can be taking for granted the things that we worked so hard to achieve, so it's wonderful to have a reminder of how far we have come.

If you are too busy to include things like this in your daily routine, then you are too busy to maintain good health, and you will make yourself sick in the long term. If you have heaped up too many responsibilities on your plate so you don't have time for yourself, devote energy to restructuring your life so you can make time. This may be a long-term project, but it's an important one. Some of us have more pressing and immediate duties than others, but no-one needs to be so busy that they never do anything for themselves.

Emotional detox is a very real thing, so be prepared. We store emotions in our cells, and a cleansing diet will give us the opportunity to release some of these limiting behaviours and belief systems. Your energy is likely to go up and down. Some days you might be feeling wiped out, in which case slow down, and watch some of the movies on the movie list (page 95). Other days you might be bouncing off the ceiling with more energy than you know what to do with, so get out there and start burning up that energy constructively, by directing it in positive ways that will strengthen and improve your physique. Whichever way you go, don't worry about it: these extreme highs and lows will pass and your energy levels will stabilise to a constant feel-good factor. Enjoy your mind and body transitioning, and observe the process without judgement; lightness of being is key to success.

Warn those close to you if you think they might end up being the recipient of some of that negative emotion! Ask them to be patient and supportive with you while you embark on this transition, and let them know that if you are unleashing anger on them, they shouldn't take it personally, it's just your over-worked liver having its say. The liver is where we store anger; kidneys is fear; spleen is resentment; gut is anxiety. If you find any of these emotions starting to rule you, consider Chinese tonic herbs as an effective way to support the organs. We have some great Chinese tonic herbal formulas on the Raw Living website, from Dragon Herbs, Shaman Shack, and Jing Herbs. I have found these traditional formulas invaluable over the years in supporting my system and keeping me in balance.

The most important thing to remember in this whole process, is that this is about you. When we understand the universe works on abundance, we understand that we must spend time and energy filling our cups up, so we have more to give. It's not about burning ourselves out trying to achieve the impossible standards of success set for us by society, and resenting everything and everyone along the way! It's about on the one hand, learning to feel happy and contented in the moment, for no other reason than you can, and on the other hand moving gracefully and with equanimity through all the challenges we experience, so that we continue to grow and expand as a human being. It's a dynamic process which demands constant awareness and attention, but it is not dependent on anyone or anything else other than this constant vigilance and commitment to your own self.

This is about you feeling good, the very best that you can feel. Enjoying the unfoldment of that relationship is fundamental to its success. And having an impeccable relationship with your body is the ultimate final result to aspire to – at the end of the day, it's not about how raw you are, it's about how amazing you can feel in your own unique skin, and how you can spread that special joy out into the world. When you die, at your funeral, no-one's going to comment on what percentage raw you were, and whether you ate potatoes that winter or drunk prosecco that summer. But they will be remembering all the wonderful things you did and all the people's lives that you touched, so make that the focus of your days, not your food choices.

Magical Living

Quantum physics teaches us that the world that we perceive as solid is actually 99% space. What is in this space? The quantum field, or the zero point field, is the true nature of reality, and the less than 1% that is perceptible to our five senses is a resulting manifestation of what is happening in this quantum field.

We imagine our thoughts to be aimlessly churning around inside our minds going nowhere, but in this quantum understanding of the universe, we realise that our thoughts are energy that exists in the field. Every thought we have is going into our own personal field or vortex, and creating our own individual reality. So we need to be mindful of where our minds travel, and encourage our thoughts into patterns that create positive and harmonious frequencies in our lives, not destructive and sabotaging ones.

As humans, we are like radio transmitters, sending and receiving signals out into the universe. As we adjust our own personal frequency, we shift the reality around us, and create the change that is needed for humanity right now.

Primary Ways To Elevate Our Energy

- Being conscious of where we put our energy and who we spend time with
- Spending time in nature
- Having a physical practice eg yoga, Thai Chi
- Having a meditation practice – 8 mins a day is a good start
- Eating raw vegan foods & staying hydrated
- Superfoods for manifestation: Cacao, Etherium Gold and Ormus Gold
- Using Tachyon devices or similar quantum technology to protect your personal energy field

Exercises for Mindfulness

- **Gratitude** – turn on the gratitude tap. What are you grateful for? Start a gratitude journal and write it in it every morning or evening. Practice with your kids.
- **Radical Self-Love** – have a daily practice of loving yourself, either in the mirror, or on your phone camera. Tell yourself how much you love you, how awesome you are, and as many good things as you can think of. Cultivate the habit of bigging yourself up in public, and not putting yourself down to others.
- **Visualisation** – use those idle, frustrating moments of modern life such as waiting for transport or being on hold on the phone, not to internally whinge and moan about life but to visualise more of what you do want. Make it a daily habit to imagine your life how you want it – the relationship, the job, the home – when you feel drawn to dwell on what is missing, use it as an opportunity to create an image of how you want it to be. Focus on the wows not the hows. This is how miracles come about.
- **Manifestation** – good givers make great getters! Think about what you want to give, not what you want to get. When you are asking for something, you are coming from a place of lack. Don't focus on material goods, especially money. The more altruistic your wishes the more power they have. The more you give unconditionally, the more the universe gives back to you in return, in unexpected ways. Protect your energy so you always have something to give.
- **The Holographic Nature of the Universe** – the world is not your mirror, that is way too simplistic, the universe is a hologram, and

the universe is love so all your lessons are compassionate. Use unwanted behaviours to look at how you can develop more compassion for yourself, and use positive reframing to turn a negative belief system into a helpful affirmation. Be mindful of the self-sabotaging belief systems you run, and see if you can get to the root of where they come from, using affirmations as a way of dissolving them.

- **Metrics for Success** – comparison is the thief of joy. Everything is relative and only you know what your path is. Define your own metrics for success. The measure of success society sets out for us, especially as women, is not attainable. Set your own definitions of what success means to you, hold yourself to them, and revisit them often.
- **You Are Enough** – less is more. Stop trying to prove anything to anyone. Think about ways you can downscale your responsibilities, do less and be more. The space you create by relaxing into who you are makes room for more joy in your life, and makes the actions you do take more productive and impactful.
- **Don't be afraid of failure.** Getting it wrong is part of the journey. It's an inevitable part of existence at this time that there will be ups and downs. The more compassion we have for ourselves, the quicker we get back on the cosmic wave. When things aren't going how you want or how you intended, see that as a valuable way to deepen your gratitude and self-love, and create an even clearer visualisation of what you do want, readying yourself to receive the next miracle.

Using Affirmations

Affirmations are powerful tools for reprogramming the subconscious. Throughout the book, I have given daily affirmations that help put your mind in a constructive, positive, loving space. You can use the ones I have given, or create your own. Repeat them as often as is needed, post them up by mirrors, light switches or the kitchen sink. You can even record yourself speaking them aloud, and then play them back to yourself. They don't even have to be audible to work, you can have them playing in the background while you are listening to music.

A really potent way to use affirmations is to have them playing while you sleep. You will find thousands of affirmation videos on YouTube, some of which are hours long.

We are programmed with belief systems of fear, lack, and inadequacy all day long by the media and by advertising, and it takes a lot of work to start undoing these unconscious scripts and have your default mindset be one of love, abundance and wholeness. Creating overall health and vitality is as much about changing our thought patterns as it is our dietary habits.

If you want to create your own affirmation, identify a limiting belief system that you have, something you find yourself repeating often, for example, "I don't have any money," or "I never have enough time." And turn that into a positive: "Money flows to me with ease," or "I find myself with always enough time to get everything done without rushing." It's important that it is in the present, and it's important that you can say it and believe it! So don't say, "I am going to be a millionaire," (which is putting it in the future), or "I am a millionaire" (which might not currently be true), but something that is meaningful to you, and allows room for growth: "I am enjoying seeing the ways in which money comes to me more readily now I am working on shifting my belief systems around it!"

Mylk Recipes

Superfood mylks are a key part of the Raw Magic lifestyle. They provide us with everything our tired bodies are craving – healthy fats, medicinal herbs, and a whole lotta hydration. I've provided you with seven recipes here – I recommend you try one a day for the first week to see what you like, and then go back to your favourites. But the choice is yours – play with them how you like – do whatever works best for you – just make sure you drink them daily! If a litre is too much for you to begin, start with 500ml, or whatever feels manageable. Use your preferred sweetener to make them sweet enough to suit your palate: personally, I use 5 drops stevia for 1 litre Mylk. I also love to use coconut water instead of spring water in my mylks. Mylk keeps in the fridge for up to 24 hours, and out of the fridge for maybe 12 hours, depending on the heat of the day, so I only recommend making as much as you are going to drink in one day. Making mylk like this shouldn't take you more than 10 minutes from start to finish, and it's way more nutritious and economical than buying plant mylk from a store.

Lucuma Blueberry Mylk

4 tbsp soaked almonds

1 tbsp lucuma

1/2 cup fresh blueberries or 1 tbsp blueberry powder

1 litre water

Add extra sweetener if desired

Soak the almonds for at least 2hrs, or overnight. Drain them, and put them in the blender with the water. Blend until smooth, then strain them through a Mylk bag. Put the almond Mylk back in the blender, along with the lucuma, blueberries, and any extra sweetener you want to use. Blend again.

Purple Chia Mylk

4 tbsp chia seeds

1/4 tsp purple corn extract

1 tsp maca

Raw honey or stevia to taste

1 litre water

Chia doesn't need soaking in advance. Put the seeds in the blender, with the purple corn, maca, sweetener and water. Blend until smooth. The chia will swell quickly and thicken the Mylk, so it's best to wait 10 mins before drinking.

Baobab Hemp Mylk

4 tbsp shelled hemp seeds

1 tbsp lecithin granules

1 tbsp Baobab

Raw honey or stevia to taste

1 litre water

Shelled hemp doesn't need soaking in advance. Blend it up with the lecithin, Baobab, sweetener and water. Hemp seeds can be a little bitter, so you will probably find you need more sweetener than some of the other recipes.

Chocolate Hemp Mylk

4 tbsp shelled hemp seeds

1 tbsp lecithin granules

2 tsp raw chocolate powder

1 tbsp cane juice crystals

1 litre water

Put everything in the blender together. Blend until smooth.

Flax Maca Mylk

4 tbsp flax seeds

1 tbsp lecithin granules

1/4 tsp Reishi extract

Raw honey or stevia to taste

1 tsp maca

1 litre water

Flax seeds don't need soaking in advance, although you can if you choose. Blend the flaxseeds, lecithin, Reishi, maca, sweetener, and water together. Reishi is quite bitter, so you may find you need more sweetener than in some of the other recipes.

Vanilla Hemp Mylk

4 tbsp whole hemp seeds

5 drops vanilla MFE

Pinch salt

1 litre water

Extra sweetener if you desire

Soak the hemp seeds in advance, for at least an hour, or overnight. Whole hemp seeds make my favourite Mylk, so it's worth the extra trouble than using shelled. Blend the hemp seeds with the water, vanilla, salt, and optional sweetener and strain using a Mylk bag.

Hazelnut Cardamom Mylk

4 tbsp hazelnuts

1 cardamom pod

1 litre water

Stevia or raw honey to taste

Soak the hazelnuts for at least 2hrs, or overnight. Drain them, and add them to the blender with the cardamom, sweetener, and water. Blend, and strain through a Mylk bag before serving.

Soak your nuts or seeds in advance, overnight if you wish, or at least an hour. Shelled hemp seeds don't need soaking. To make your Mylk, blend up the nuts or seeds in the water, and then strain through a Mylk bag (chia, flax and shelled hemp don't need straining). Pour the Mylk back in the blender with all the other ingredients and give it another whizz.

Green Juice Recipes

Green juice is so important! Maybe the most important thing in the plan. Even if you're deviating from your set meal times, try and make sure you get your green juice and your superfood Mylks in and you'll still be progressing wonderfully. Drinking super-nutritional drinks in large quantities is the best way to retrain the body into craving healthy foods. If it's too much for you in the beginning, you can make up a recipe and drink half of it one day, half the next, but I really recommend trying to drink it all in one day if you can.

The use of Green Juice for healing was pioneered by Ann Wigmore of the Hippocrates Health Institute. The Hippocrates Method involves no fruit, as they believe even the natural sugars found in fruits are a significant contributory factor in disease. You will find the green juice recipes given below also don't contain any sweet fruits. Lemon and grapefruit are the two most alkalizing fruits, so we include those. If these recipes really are not to your taste, you can add an apple or a pear, but I hope that I've made the recipes so tasty as they are, that you don't feel that you need to. Adding some coconut water is another good way to increase the sweet taste, while still keeping the juice alkalizing.

Makes 500ml-750ml juice, depending on size of your cucumbers

If you use the blender method given below, it takes 10-20 mins to make your juice, including clean-up time

Green Juice Recipe One

1 cucumber
1/2 head celery
1 lemon
1 clove garlic
50g spinach

Green Juice Recipe Two

1 cucumber
1/2 head celery
1 lime
25g parsley
10g turmeric root

Green Juice Recipe Three

1 cucumber
1/2 head celery
50g kale
1 lemon
10g ginger root

Green Juice Recipe Four

1 cucumber
1/2 head celery
1/2 ruby grapefruit
50g spinach
10g ginger root
10g turmeric root

Green Juice Recipe Five

1 cucumber
1/2 head celery
1 head fennel
1 lemon

Green Juice Recipe Six

1 cucumber
1/2 head celery
1 lime
2 lime leaves
1 stick lemongrass
50g spinach

Green Juice Recipe Seven

1 cucumber
1/2 head celery
4 lettuce leaves
1/2 ruby grapefruit
1 clove garlic
10g ginger root

I prefer the blender method when it comes to making juice.

1. It's time-saving
2. You don't need to invest in an expensive piece of equipment
3. You don't need to find space in your kitchen for a large piece of equipment.
4. You don't need to wash the juicer afterwards!

A high power blender helps, but a standard high street blender will do the job as well. Chop all your veg small enough for your blender to handle. Put the cucumber and lemons in first, and blend those to a soup. You don't need to blend them too long, it doesn't need to be smooth yet. Then add in your other ingredients, in stages if you're blender isn't so powerful, or all at once if you've got a good machine. Blend again until smooth. Have your Mylk bag ready over a bowl, and pour the pulp into the bag so it starts draining into the bowl. If you can hang the bag up, it can be dripping while you are washing up the blender and cleaning away your veg scraps. Squeeze the remaining juice out, and you are done.

Only make as much juice as you are going to drink in a day. Keep it in the fridge if you are not going to drink it all straight away.

Leftover pulp can be fed to dogs, or added to cracker or bread recipes. It freezes well if you want to reserve it for later use.

Breakfast Recipes

Raw breakfasts don't come out of a packet (well, they do at a price!). You're going to need to invest some time in pre-prep to make your breakfasts work. However, this is all done in advance, so don't worry, you can still hit the snooze button a few times before making it down to the kitchen. The cereal, crackers and chocolate spread recipes make enough to last you a full week. The chia you're going to have to make more mid-week, but that only takes a few minutes. And the oats just need a little attention before you go to bed each night.

Cereal

Serves 4. You can double this & make enough to last a week.

Takes 5 mins

2 cups (250g) buckwheaties

1/2 cup (50g) shelled hemp seeds

1/2 cup (50g) raisins

1 tbsp maca

Buckwheaties are the soaked, sprouted, dehydrated buckwheat groats, you can make your own or buy them ready-made from Raw Living.

Mix everything together. Store in an airtight container, keeps fine. Serve with your Mylk of choice: I recommend almond or hemp. Use 2-4 tbsp per litre of water, and strain through a Mylk bag for the most economical and freshest Mylk.

Chia Porridge

Makes 4 servings

Takes 5 mins, with soaking for at least one hour

150g (1 cup) chia

1 litre (4 cups) Mylk of choice

1/2 cup (50g) lucuma

1 cup fresh fruit

1 tbsp tahini

1 tbsp raw honey

Combine everything together in a large 2 litre serving bowl, whisking it up with a fork to ensure there are no lumps in the chia. Use whichever fresh fruit is in season: berries are good in the summer, finely chopped apples and pears in the winter. Leave to soak for at least an hour, so the seeds swell up and absorb all of the Mylk. Store in a glass container. Will keep in the fridge up to 5 days.

Oats

Use about 100g per serving.

Takes 5 mins

Use about 100g per serving. Soak overnight in 1 cup (250ml) of your Mylk of choice. In the morning add whatever makes your heart sing e.g. chopped fresh fruit, dried fruit, cacao powder, tahini, maca. I used to love miso porridge in the winter, for a warming, satisfying, nurturing start to the day. If you want your porridge heated, you can add a little hot water before you serve it.

Goji Crackers

Makes 50 crackers

**Soaking time 4-8 hrs,
dehydrating time 18-24 hrs**

2 cups (150g) flaxseeds

1/2 cup (50g) raisins or goji berries

1 tbsp cinnamon powder

Soaked 4-8 hrs in 4 cups (1 litre) pure water

In a large 2 litre mixing bowl, put the flax and water, and add 1/2 - 1 cup dried fruit e.g. gojis, raisins, mulberries, and the cinnamon. Leave for 4-8 hours to soak. When you're ready, spread the mixture over 2 dehydrator trays. Dehydrate it for approx. 12 hrs. Then score into crackers, 25 per sheet (5 across, 5 down), using a knife or scissors. Flip the crackers, and dry another 6-12 hrs, until crispy. Store in an airtight container (they don't need refrigeration).

Chocolate Spread

Makes 8 servings

Takes 5 mins

2 tbsp tahini

2 tbsp coconut nectar or raw honey

1 tbsp raw cacao powder

1 tbsp hemp or flax oil

In a small mixing bowl, mix everything together with a spoon. Don't eat it all at once! If you are that kind of person, maybe make double ☺. Store in a jar in the fridge, keeps well for a few weeks. This is for spreading on your crackers but it also makes good icing for cakes.

Chia Crackers

Lunch Recipes

These recipes should all take under 20 mins to prepare. They all suit being made the night before and taken out with you as a packed lunch if needs be. Remember, the point of this 28-day programme is to have you feeling more well-nourished than you have ever done in your life before! It's not a starvation programme. So eat as much as you want of these life-affirming foods. It's likely that after a few weeks or even a few days, as your appetite adjusts, you will find yourself enjoying smaller portions than what you started with. It's important not to restrict yourself, but to eat to your heart's content.

Guacamole

Serves 2

Takes 15 mins

2 avocados

1 tomato

1 tbsp hemp oil

1 tbsp tahini

Juice 1/2 lemon

Pinch crystal salt

1/4 tsp cayenne pepper

Sprinkle hemp seeds, cacao nibs or bee pollen

Remove the flesh from the avocados and transfer it to a small mixing bowl. Finely dice the tomato. Juice the lemon, add the hemp oil, tahini salt and cayenne, and mash it all together with a fork. I like it with texture like this; if you put it in the blender it goes more into a pudding. Sprinkle with something crunchy e.g. shelled hemp seeds, to give it bite. Store it in the fridge in an airtight glass container. Guac only keeps as well as your avocados: 3-4 days if you're lucky, one day if you're not.

Turmeric Butter

Serves 2

Takes 5 mins

2 tbsp tahini

1 tsp miso

1/2 tsp mustard

2 tbsp hemp oil

1 tsp apple cider vinegar

1 tsp turmeric powder

Water to mix

I eat this a lot! I put it on crackers, mash it up with avocado to make scrambled "egg", thin it out and use it as cheese on pizza or nachos. If you're using it as butter, you need less water, but if you're using it as a dip you may need as much as 1/4 cup water. Put all the ingredients in a small mixing bowl and mix together using a spoon. Store in a glass jar in the fridge, keeps well, up to a few weeks.

Stuffed Avocado

(Original recipe in Eat Smart, Eat Raw)
Serves 2

Takes 15 mins, with pre-soaking 1-2 hrs

60 g (1/2 cup) sunflower and/or pumpkin seeds, pre-soaked

1 carrot, chopped

6 sun-dried tomatoes

1 tsp miso

30 g alfalfa sprouts

2 avocados

Pre-soak your seeds 2-4 hrs. If you soak your sun-dried tomatoes for an hour in advance, it will soften them, and help them break down easier in the food processor. Prepare your carrots. Drain the seeds, and add them to the food processor with the carrots, sun-dried tomatoes, and miso. Process until you have a thick puree. If you want, you can double this stage of the recipe and have some spare pâté for another day.

Next, slice the avocados in half and remove the stones. Then fill the holes where the stones were with the carrot mixture, and cover the flesh with a thin layer. Top with alfalfa sprouts, to cover each half. Serve immediately, with a spoon.

Stuffed Avocado

Kale Chips

Serves 4

Takes 15 mins, with up to 12 hrs dehydrating

500g (1/2 lb) kale

1/4 cup (25g) tahini

1/4 cup (60 ml) olive oil

1 tbsp apple cider vinegar

1/4 tsp salt

1/2 tsp chilli powder

1/3 cup (80 ml) water

First, prepare your kale for the dehydrator. Tear it into pieces (not too small as kale shrinks a lot in the dehydrator, tearing each leaf into two or three should be fine), and remove any large stems which will be indigestible if dehydrated. Put it in a large 2 litre bowl. Then in a small bowl, stir together all the other ingredients. Put everything together in the bowl – tahini, olive oil, vinegar, salt and chilli. Mix together well, then gradually add the water, until you have a thick pouring sauce. Pour it over the kale, and stir together so the kale is evenly coated. Don't massage it in, just make sure it's covering the kale nicely. Spread over two dehydrating trays and dry for up to 12 hrs. They are ready when they are all crispy, with no soggy bits left. If you haven't got a dehydrator, you can make these in the oven – gas 4, electric (350°F or 175°C) for 10-15 mins.

Tomato Salad

Serves one

Takes 10 mins

3 tomatoes

10g fresh basil

1 tbsp hemp oil

1 tsp balsamic vinegar

Pinch crystal salt

Chop the tomatoes into quarters. Fine chop the basil into tiny pieces. Mix everything together. Serve immediately.

Courgette Hummus

Makes 8 servings

Takes 15 mins

1 cup (125g) sesame seeds

2 courgette

1 tbsp tahini

1 lemon, juiced

1/3 cup (80 ml) olive oil

1 clove garlic

Pinch cayenne

Pinch salt

No-one ever guesses that this is not chickpea hummus! Peel the courgette first to make the hummus less bitter and more smooth. Chop them up, then just blend everything together until creamy. Store in the fridge in a glass container, will keep for up to a week..

Bayonnaise

Makes 8 servings

Takes 10 mins, with at least 2hrs pre-soaking

1 cup (100g) sunflower seeds, soaked 2 – 4 hrs

1 tbsp Baobab powder

2 tbsp olive oil

1/2 cup (125 ml) water

Pinch salt

Pre-soak your sunflower seeds for at least 2 hrs. Don't soak them too long or they will go bitter and spoil the flavour of your mayo. When you're ready, drain them, and blend them with all the other ingredients, to a smooth creamy consistency. Store in the fridge in a glass container for up to a week. I use this on everything! As a dip, as a butter on crackers, in nori wraps, as a salad dressing, as a sauce on kelp noodles, and more.

Chia Crackers

Makes about 20 large crackers

Needs 4 hrs pre-soaking and 18-24 hrs dehydrating

1 cup (100g) sunflower seeds

1/2 cup (50g) pumpkin seeds

1 cup (125g) chia seeds

1 cup (25g) dulse flakes

1/2 cup (60g) sesame seeds

1/2 tsp crystal salt

1 tsp honey

5 cups (1.25 litres) water

Put all your ingredients, every single one, into a large 2 litre mixing bowl together. Give it a good stir, so all the flavourings are equally distributed, and leave to soak for 4-8hrs. When you're ready, spread the mixture over 2 dehydrator sheets & dry for approx 12 hrs. Score into 25 crackers (5 up by 5 down), either with a knife or scissors, and flip the individual crackers. Dry for another 6-12 hours. Store in an airtight container, will keep indefinitely.

Bayonnaise

Pumpkin Seed Pâté

Makes 8 servings

Takes 15 mins, with at least 2hrs pre-soaking

1 cup (60g) sun-dried tomatoes

1 clove garlic

1/4 red onion

1 tbsp tamari

1/2 cup (125 ml) olive oil

1 cup (250ml) water

1 cup (125g) pumpkin seeds soaked 2-4hrs

1 romaine lettuce

Pre-soak the pumpkin seeds for at least 2 hrs. I recommend using Austrian pumpkin seeds, such as the ones you can get from Raw Living, not Chinese, there is a big difference. When you're ready, drain your pumpkin seeds. To leave it with a bit of texture, rather than have it completely smooth and creamy, blend everything apart from the pumpkin seeds first, then when you have a thick batter, include the pumpkin seeds. Once it's blended, tear off some large romaine (cos) lettuce leaves and fill your leaf with around 1/2 cup of the mixture. You can add some extra beansprouts or salad greens if you have some knocking around. Roll up the mixture inside the leaf, and serve with the wrapped edge underneath. Any leftover pate can be stored in an airtight container in the fridge, will keep for up to a week. Remove from the blender and store in an airtight glass container in the fridge, will keep for up to a week.

Hemp Tabbouleh

Serves four

Takes 15 mins

1 1/4 cups (150g) shelled hemp seeds

500g (2 cups) tomatoes

1/2 cucumber

25g fresh mint leaves

100g fresh parsley

1 lemon, juiced

4 tbsp olive oil

Pinch salt

Dice the tomatoes and cucumber. Put them in a large 2 litre salad bowl, along with the hemp seeds. Finely mince the parsley and mint leaves, as fine as you can. Add the lemon juice, olive oil, and salt, and give it a good mix. I like mine lemony; if you do too, you may want to add an extra juiced lemon. It is best to let it marinate 30 minutes before serving. Keeps well in the fridge, up to 5 days.

Hummus, Falafel & Hemp Tabbouleh

Sunshine Soup

(Original recipe in Eat Smart, Eat Raw)
Serves 2
Takes 20 mins

3 tomatoes
1 yellow pepper
1/2 avocado
60 g (2 oz) baby leaf spinach
250 ml (8 fl oz) almond Mylk
1 tbsp flaxseed oil
1 tsp miso
10g ginger root
1 clove garlic

Prepare your tomatoes, pepper, and spinach for the blender. Put everything apart from the avocado in the blender, and puree until all you have a smooth, lump-free soup. Add the avocado last, and give it a quick whizz so its smooth. If you want to warm it, stand the soup in a heat-proof bowl in a pan of gently simmering water. If you are blessed with a Thermomix, heat it at 45° for 10 minutes.

Cucumber Salad

Serves two
Takes 10 mins

2 avocados
1 cucumber
1 tbsp flax oil
Pinch crystal salt
1 tbsp Salad Topping (see below)

Cube the avocados into bite-sized pieces and spoon out the flesh into a mixing bowl. Cube the cucumber into pieces the same size and add them to the bowl. Stir in the flax oil and crystal salt. It's nice with a topping like Rawmesan, Engevita, Salad Booster, or my Super Salad Sprinkle.

Cauliflower Cheese

(Original recipe in Eat Smart Eat Raw)
Serves 2
Takes 15 mins (extra dehydration time optional)

250 g (about half) cauliflower, divided into bite-sized florets
4 tbsp tahini
1 tsp tamari
1 lemon, juiced
2 tbsp water
2 tbsp nutritional yeast flakes

Put all the ingredients except the cauliflower in a bowl and blend together with a hand whisk. Pour over cauliflower, toss and serve. If you have a dehydrator, and you have time, you can put this in for a few hours to warm and soften.

Mediterranean Salad

Serves 2

Takes 20 mins

1 romaine lettuce

250g (8 oz) cherry tomatoes

1/2 cucumber

1 yellow pepper

200 g (7 oz) pitted olives

4 tbsp extra virgin olive oil

1 tbsp balsamic vinegar

1/4 tsp rock salt

1 tsp smoked paprika

Halve the tomatoes, finely dice the cucumbers and peppers, and tear the lettuce. Add the olives, and give everything a good toss in the dressing ingredients. If you're craving cooked food, this salad works well with the addition of some baby new potatoes.

Sauerkraut Slaw

Serves four

Takes 20 mins

1 avocado

1/2 lemon, juiced

1/2 tsp cayenne

1 tsp tamari

2 carrots

1/4 red onion

300g sauerkraut

Blend the avocado, lemon juice, cayenne and tamari together to make the dressing. Grate the carrots and onion finely. I love purple carrots the best! Mix everything together. Keeps well in the fridge, up to 5 days.

Muhammara

Serves 4

Takes 15 mins, with 4hrs pre-soaking

1 cup (100g) walnuts, soaked for 4 hrs

2 red peppers

1 tsp honey or coconut nectar

1/2 tsp cayenne pepper

2 tsp smoked paprika

1/4 tsp salt

1 lemon, juiced

4 tbsp olive oil

Pre-soak the walnuts and when they are ready drain them, then put them in the blender with all the other ingredients. Blend til smooth, then store in the fridge for up to five days.

Carrot & Spinach Soup

(Original recipe in Raw Living)

Serves 2

Takes 20 mins

250g (3) carrots

100 g baby leaf spinach

1 clove garlic

1 avocado

1 tsp miso

1 tbsp flaxseed oil

1 tsp kelp powder

1 tsp turmeric powder

250 ml (1 cup) hot water

50 g (1 cup) mung bean sprouts

Prepare the carrots, spinach, garlic and avocado for the blender. Put all your ingredients in, apart from the sprouts and puree until smooth. Mix the sprouts in by hand - sprinkle a few on the top as a garnish.

Kimchi Salad

Serves two

Takes 10 mins

200g (1 cup) Kimchi

100g (2 cups) mung bean sprouts

1 head bok choy

For the dressing:

50g ginger root

2 tbsp sesame oil

1 tbsp rice vinegar

1 tsp honey or coconut nectar

1 tsp miso

Fine slice the bok choy. In a large 2 litre mixing bowl, stir the Kimchi, bean sprouts, and bok choy together. Mix them together with a fork.

To make the dressing, chop the ginger finely and add it to the blender with the other ingredients. Blend for a minute until you've eliminated all the ginger chunks, or as many as possible.

Pour the dressing over the salad and enjoy straight away or let it marinade and eat it the next day. Keeps in the fridge for a couple of days.

Ramen

(Original recipe on KateMagic.com)

Serves two

Takes 20 mins

Broth:

500ml water

1 red chilli pepper

10g ginger root

1 garlic clove

1 tsp cane juice crystals

1 tsp miso paste

1 tsp tamari

1 tsp rice vinegar

Noodles:

1 courgette

100g mung bean sprouts

10g wakame, soaked

50g kimchi

Garnish:

2 tbsp cold-pressed sesame oil

First, spiralise your courgette, and soak your wakame in a bowl of warm water. Then, it's time to make your broth. Deseed the chilli carefully (and wash your hands with hot soapy water afterwards!). Peel the garlic clove. Put everything in the blender together: chilli, ginger, garlic, sugar, miso, tamari, and rice vinegar. Heat the water in the kettle; I use a temperature control kettle that means the water doesn't reach boiling point, I would say 80 deg C or 180 F is around optimum. If your water boils, I would let it cool a little first before you use it, so it's not too hot to the touch. When you're ready, add the water to the jug, and give it all a good whizz together. Make sure all the chilli and garlic are blended up well.

Pour out the broth into two bowls; wide shallow bowls are best in order to show off the constituent ingredients or everything can get over-crowded. Take your noodles and place them in the broth. Place the accompanying ingredients alongside the noodles; the beansprouts, seaweed and Kimchi. You can play around and add whatever vegetables or seaweeds take your fancy; I do lots of variations on this recipe. Drip the sesame oil over the top so it makes pretty bubbles in the broth. Serve immediately while it's warm.

Dinner Recipes

These all take around 30 mins or less to prepare. Everything is vegan and gluten-free. We start off with some wholesome vegan semi-raw meals; these are the kind of things you should fall back on when the high raw is getting too much. Remember, it's always more helpful to focus on having a balanced wholefoods diet than focus on raw (or vegan) to the exclusion of everything else.

I have kept the recipes as simple as possible, because I don't want to overwhelm you with lots of ingredients. Feel free to add your own favourite spice blends or superfoods. I love using a little turmeric powder, kelp powder, and our Raw Living 14 mushroom blend to add flavor and nutrition to my dishes. Sometimes I add a sprinkle of E3 Blue Majik, or a pinch of Harmonic Innerprizes Aulterra (both available from the Raw Living website). Another top tip is smothering whatever you have made in some fermented hot sauce, such as the one made by The Urban Fermentery.

Many of these recipes are simplified versions of ones that appear in my books and my website, particularly the book Eat Smart Eat Raw. This is the book I always recommend for beginners, and you may find it helpful to purchase that book as well for added inspiration.

Please note, most recipes serve two, as I'm assuming that you're not eating alone. If you are, you can make extra and save it for another day, or simply half the amounts given.

Green Salad with Baked Sweet Potato

Serves 2

Takes 45 mins to bake the potato and 10 mins to make the salad

2 sweet potatoes

1 tbsp coconut oil

100g (4 oz) salad pack

1/2 red pepper

1/2 cucumber

1 avocado

2 tbsp hemp oil

Pinch crystal salt

2 tsp balsamic vinegar

Heat the oven to 200°C/ Gas 6. Pierce the potatoes with a fork. Put them in a baking tray lined with foil (you can brush them with some coconut oil if you like, to make the skins crispy). Bake for 45 minutes.

While they are baking, prepare your salad. Dice pepper, cucumber and avocado and add to the salad pack. Add your hemp oil, salt and vinegar.

Serve the potato with coconut oil or olive oil drizzled over, and extra salt and pepper, along with the salad. Never underestimate the power of those obvious dishes, such as this one! You can't fail with a big green salad.

Arame & Quinoa Salad

Serves 2

Takes 20 mins

1 cup (125g) quinoa

2 1/2 cups (625ml) water

1 carrot, grated

1 red pepper, diced

1/2 cup arame, soaked 15 mins

2 tbsp tahini

1 tbsp olive oil

Juice 1 lemon

1 tsp tamari

Water to blend

Put the quinoa and water in a saucepan together. Bring to the boil, and then let it simmer for just 15 mins. Turn the heat off and let it stand for a further 5 mins. While that's cooking, pre-soak the arame. Grate the carrot, and dice the red pepper. Make a dressing by stirring together the tahini, lemon juice, olive oil and tamari. The lemon juice acts as a coagulant, so you will need a tablespoon or two of water to get it to the right consistency for a dressing. Once the quinoa is cooked, put half aside for tomorrow. Drain the arame and add it to the quinoa, along with the veggies and the dressing. Enjoy warm.

Millet & Spinach Salad

Serves 2

Takes 20 mins

1 cup (125g) millet

2 1/2 cups (625 ml) water

1/4 cucumber, diced

2 tomatoes, diced

100g baby leaf spinach

2 tbsp flax oil

1 tsp apple cider vinegar

1 tsp miso

Put the millet and water in a saucepan together. Bring the water to the boil, then let it simmer for just 15 mins. Turn the heat off, and let it stand for a further 15 mins. While it's cooking, prepare the cucumber and tomatoes, by dicing them finely. Once the millet is cooked, stir in your veggies and the dressing ingredients. Enjoy warm (leftovers can be enjoyed cold the next day).

Tempeh Stir Fry

Serves 2

Takes 20 mins

2 cloves garlic

10g ginger root

1/2 red onion

1 carrot

100g (1 cup) cabbage

1 red pepper

2 tbsp cashew nuts

100g Tempeh

2 tbsp coconut oil

1 tbsp tamari

1 lime, juiced

Mince the garlic and ginger. Fine slice all your veggies: a mandolin is good for this if you have one, or the slicing blade on a food processor; otherwise just get them as thin as you can. Chop your Tempeh into cubes. Heat the oil in a wok or frying pan and tip all the veggies, cashews and Tempeh in. Fry for as little time as possible! A few minutes should be enough. Season with tamari and lime.

Tahini Kale Salad

Serves 2

Takes 15 mins

200g kale

2 tbsp olive oil

1/4 tsp salt

1 tbsp tahini

1 tsp balsamic vinegar

1/2 tsp smoked paprika

50g alfalfa sprouts

Tear the kale into small pieces, removing any thick stalks. Massage the oil and salt into the kale. Keep massaging until the kale starts getting squishy – this will take a few minutes. Add the tahini, vinegar and paprika; you will probably need to use your hands again to make sure the tahini coats the kale. Stir in the alfalfa sprouts. Keeps well, up to five days in the fridge.

Roasted Veggies

Serves 2

Takes 15 mins to make, plus 45 mins roasting time

1/4 butternut squash (approx. 200g)

1 red onion

2 courgettes

1tbsp coconut oil

1 tsp tamari

1 tbsp dried mixed herbs

To prepare your roast veggies, chop the squash, onion and courgette into medium sized chunks, mix evenly, and place in a baking tray lined with foil. Pour the coconut oil, tamari and herbs over. Bake in a pre-heated oven (200°C/400°F/gas mark 6) for around 45 minutes.

Reuben's Tomato Soup

Serves two
Takes 15 mins

5 tomatoes
10g parsley
2 red peppers
2 pickled beetroot or 1 raw beetroot
1 red chilli pepper
200g cauliflower
2 tbsp olive oil
Pinch salt

Prepare your tomatoes, parsley, peppers, and cauliflower for your blender. Cooked beetroot is easier to blend and also adds an acidic flavour element, raw beetroot is good as well, but will just need a little more blending. Remove the seeds from the chilli pepper (and wash your hands with soap afterwards!). Blend everything together to a nice chunky consistency; not lumpy but not pureed either. Transfer to a pan and heat gently, so it's warmed but not boiled.

Authentic Bread

(Original recipe on KateMagic.com)
Makes 8-12 slices
Takes 15 mins to make, 12 hrs to dehydrate

2 cups flaxseeds
1/2 cup psyllium powder
2 tbsp tamari
4 tbsp extra virgin olive oil
1 tbsp baobab powder
1 tbsp turmeric powder
1 tbsp cane juice crystals
1 tbsp apple cider vinegar
1/4 tsp black pepper
1/4 tsp cayenne powder
2 cups water

Grind your flaxseeds in a high power blender or food grinder. Transfer them to a mixing bowl, and add in the dry ingredients: psyllium, baobab, turmeric, cane juice crystals, black pepper, and cayenne. Mix thoroughly with a spoon or by hand.

Then add the liquid ingredients: the tamari, olive oil, and apple cider vinegar, and mix again. Lastly stir in the water until you have a firm dough. It's probably easiest to do this by hand.

Press the dough into a loaf shape on your dehydrator sheet. You don't want the bread to be more than 1" (2-3cm high) or it won't dry through properly. Put it in the dehydrator and dry it for 8-12 hours, then flip and dry for another 2-4 hours on the other side.

Store in an airtight container in the fridge. Will keep for up to a week.

Honey Roasted Parsnips with Rocket Salad

Serves 2

Takes 15 mins to make, plus 30 mins roasting time

4 parsnips

2 tbsp coconut oil

1 tsp honey or coconut nectar

100g rocket

1 tbsp extra virgin olive oil

1 tbsp balsamic vinegar

6 cherry tomatoes

To roast the parsnips, pre-heat oven to (200°C/400°F/gas mark 6). Slice the parsnips in quarters lengthways, and place them in a baking tray. Pour the coconut oil and honey over and cook for 20-30 mins.

To make the salad, simply half the cherry tomatoes and place them in a bowl with the rocket and toss in the olive oil and balsamic vinegar. Serve immediately.

Marinara Pasta Sauce

(Original recipe in Eat Smart Eat Raw)

Serves 2

Takes 20 mins

3 tomatoes

1/2 avocado

2 carrots

1 stick celery

6 sun-dried tomatoes

1 fresh date

2 tbsp extra virgin olive oil

1 tsp tamari

1 tsp apple cider vinegar

1 clove garlic

1/2 red chilli pepper

The most used recipe in my repertoire! Been making this for over 20 years and it's still going strong. Prepare the tomatoes, avocado, carrots and celery for the blender. If your sun-dried tomatoes are very dry, you may find it helps to soak them in water for an hour first. De-seed the chilli (wash your hands with soapy water afterwards!). Put everything in the blender and blend to a thick sauce. Pour over your favourite brand of organic gluten-free pasta, there are many to choose from. If you want to go fully raw, spiralise a courgette and use that instead of pasta.

Spinach & Potato Curry

Serves 2

Takes 25 mins

250g (8 oz) potatoes

3 tomatoes

1 carrot

1 red pepper

2 tbsp coconut oil

curry spices/paste to taste

pinch salt

1 tbsp apple cider vinegar

100g baby leaf spinach

Cook potatoes by cubing them, and putting them in a pan of water. Bring to the boil, and then simmer for 15 mins. Make a raw tomato curry sauce by blending tomatoes, carrot, red pepper, coconut oil, vinegar, salt and curry flavouring. Transfer to a large mixing bowl, and stir the spinach into the curry. Drain the potatoes and stir those in also. Serve while potatoes are still hot, and you would never guess it wasn't a fully cooked meal!

Steamed Broccoli with Coleslaw

Serves 2

Takes 20 mins

250g (8 oz) broccoli

2 tbsp shelled hemp seeds

2 tbsp extra virgin olive oil

2 carrots

200 g white cabbage

1/2 red onion

2 tbsp vegan mayonnaise

Chop the broccoli into florets. Place in a steamer basket and steam for 5-10 minutes. Transfer to a bowl, and sprinkle with shelled hemp and olive oil. To make the slaw, grate or fine slice the carrots, cabbage and onions, then toss with the mayo. Add salt and pepper to taste.

Coleslaw (Made with Purple Carrots)

Thai Yellow Curry

(Original recipe in Eat Smart Eat Raw)
Serves 2

Takes 20 mins

2 tomatoes

1 yellow pepper

1 carrot

1 date

2 tbsp lecithin granules

2 tbsp coconut oil

1 tsp apple cider vinegar

1 tsp turmeric powder

1 tsp yellow curry paste

1 tsp tamari

4 mushrooms

100g baby spinach leaves

To make the sauce, first prepare your tomatoes, pepper, carrot and date for the blender. Put them all in together and give them a quick whiz. Then add the lecithin, coconut oil, apple cider vinegar, turmeric, curry paste and tamari and blend again until smooth. Transfer to a large mixing bowl. Fine slice your mushrooms and add that into the bowl. Tip in your baby spinach leaves, and stir those in. Serve immediately. Doesn't keep well, eat within 24 hours.

Stuffed Avo & Spinach Salad

(Original Recipe in Raw Living)
Serves 2

Takes 15 mins

1/4 cup (25g) goji berries (or sun-dried tomatoes)

1/4 cup (10g) coconut flakes

1 stick celery

5g ginger root

Pinch salt

1/2 cup cauliflower

1 tbsp tahini

2 avocados

25g alfalfa sprouts

2 tbsp olive oil

1 tbsp tahini

2 tbsp maca

1 tsp miso

100 g or 2 cups spinach

To make the stuffing for the avocado, put the goji berries, coconut flakes, celery, ginger, salt, tahini and cauliflower into a food processor and blend for a minute. It doesn't need to be smooth, it's better with a bit of texture. Slice the avos in half and remove the stones. Spoon the stuffing onto the avos, and cover each half with the alfalfa sprouts.

To make the spinach salad, blend the olive oil, tahini, maca and miso together in a small bowl or a cup, then pour it over the spinach and toss. If you want to use your hands, you can massage the sauce into the spinach and it will wilt like it does when it's cooked.

Instant Pizza

Serves 2

Takes 25 mins

4-6 crackers

Marinara (Page 76)

100g mixed chopped veg (see below)

2 tbsp olive oil

1 tsp tamari

1 tsp Balsamic vinegar

1 tsp dried oregano

1 tsp dried thyme

First of all, marinade the veg of your choice in the olive oil, tamari, vinegar and herbs. I love kale or spinach pizza. You can also add olives, mushrooms, sweetcorn, red peppers, capers, artichoke hearts, whatever you love. Dice it all up and leave it in the marinade while you make your tomato sauce (page 76). Take some ready-made raw crackers or bread (eg Wrawps Pizza Bases or Raw Health Intensely Italian crispbreads). Spread with your marinade, then heap the vegetables on top. If you want to add cheese, use the turmeric butter recipe from page 62 and drizzle it over the top.

Falafel

Makes about 20

(Original recipe in Eat Smart Eat Raw)

2 cups (250 g) pumpkin seeds or walnuts (soaked)

1 cup sun-dried tomatoes

2 tbsp tahini

60 ml (1/4 cup) extra virgin olive oil

60 ml (1/4 cup) water

1 tsp tamari

2 lemons, juiced

1 bunch (25g) fresh coriander

2 cloves garlic

1/4 red onion

2 tsp ground cumin

1 tsp honey or coconut nectar

Soak your nuts or seeds for at least 4 hrs before you start. Put everything in the blender, and puree for a few minutes until the mixture is a smooth batter. Place tablespoons of the mixture onto a dehydrating sheet, about 2 cm (1") high. Dehydrate for about 18 hours.

These are tricky to make without a dehydrator. You can try omitting the water and making them in the food processor instead of the blender, so the mixture is less liquid and sticks together more. Then roll them into balls by hand. You could cheat and shallow fry them, or grill them, so they are heated without cooking them through.

Serve with the leftover hemp tabbouleh from yesterday.

Umami Kale & Kelp Noodles
(Original recipe on KateMagic.com)
Serves 2
Takes 20 mins

1 pkt (340g) kelp noodles
1 lemon, juiced
1 tbsp tamari
50g (2 oz) kale
2 tbsp extra virgin olive oil
1/2 tsp salt
2 tbsp pumpkin seed butter
2 tbsp hemp oil
1 tsp apple cider vinegar
2 tbsp water
100g (1/2c) Mixed beansprouts

Rinse the kelp noodles well in warm water. Chop them up with scissors. Put them in a bowl with the juice of one lemon and 1T tamari. Massage the noodles in the marinade, as if you're making sauerkraut. Within a minute, they will change texture and become very soft. Leave them in the marinade while you make the rest of the dish.

Tear the kale into small pieces, and put them in a separate bowl with the olive oil and salt. Your kale also needs massaging (don't we all!). Spend a few minutes breaking it down with your hands, so it's edible and lost its crunch.

Make your dressing in a small bowl, by mixing the pumpkin seed butter, hemp oil, apple cider vinegar, and water. Stir it up with a spoon.

Now you're ready to assemble the dish. Drain the marinade from the kelp noodles (I pour it off and store it in a jar in the fridge, to add it into a cracker batter, it's a shame to throw it out). In a large bowl, mix the kelp noodles, kale, beansprouts, and dressing. Mix it thoroughly and it's ready to serve.

Leftovers can be stored in the fridge in an airtight container, and keep well, for up to a week.

Umami Kale

Nori Tacos

Serves 2

Takes 30 mins

4 nori sheets

Marinara sauce (pre-prepped from yesterday)

1 cup walnuts (pre-soaked)

Sour cream:

1 cup (125g) shelled hemp seeds

1 tbsp baobab powder

2 tbsp olive oil

1 lemon, juiced

pinch salt

1 cup (250ml) water

Pre-soak the walnuts for at least an hour, preferably 4 hrs. Get your marinara sauce out of the fridge, that you pre-prepped yesterday. Using a food processor, grind the walnuts to the consistency of mincemeat. Transfer the sauce and nuts into a mixing bowl, stir them together and leave to stand. Make the sour cream by putting the hemp, baobab, olive oil, lemon juice, salt and water in the blender together and blending for a minute until creamy.

Make your taco shell by folding your nori sheets in half, and cutting them into the shape of taco shells by cutting a semi-circle shape. You can also use a large romaine lettuce leaf. Fill your taco shell with the tomato mixture, and pour a little cream on top. Serve two tacos per person. Save leftover sour cream for the Sea Spaghetti recipe on page 84, or use as a dip or spread.

Beet It Soup

(Original Recipe in Raw Living)

Serves 2

Takes 20 mins

2 raw beetroots

1 carrot

3 tomatoes

1 red chilli pepper

2 dates

2 tbsp extra virgin olive oil

1 tsp tamari

250 ml (1 cup) water

1 tbsp dulse flakes

Top, tail and peel the beetroot. Chop into blender-friendly pieces. Top, tail and chop the carrot, and cut the tomatoes into quarters. Seed the red chilli, pit the dates. Put all your prepared veg in the blender, along with the olive oil and tamari (put the tomatoes in first, at the bottom, to make it easy for your blender). Blend for a couple of minutes until you're satisfied there's no lumpy bits left. Pour into bowls and sprinkle with the dulse.

Serve with raw bread or crackers. You can also spread your bread with Turmeric Butter (Page 62) for a real treat.

Broccoli & Mushroom Curry

Serves 2

Takes 15 mins

3 tomatoes

1 carrots

1/2 red peppers

1 stick celery

2 tbsp coconut oil

1 tsp apple cider vinegar

1 tsp tamari

1 date

1 tsp curry paste

50g (2 oz) broccoli

50g (2oz) green beans

25g (1 oz) mushrooms

Prep your veg for the blender. Blend everything together apart from the broccoli, beans and mushrooms. Dice those, and pour the blended sauce over the veg. If you want to warm this gently, it brings out the flavours. Put it in a heatproof bowl in pan of simmering water, or it works really well in a Thermomix if you have one.

Cauliflower Rice

Serves 4

Takes 15 mins

1 cauliflower (500g or 1/2 lb)

1 cup (100g) sesame seeds

1 cup (50g) coconut chips

1 tbsp tamari

4 tbsp sesame oil

1 tbsp rice vinegar

1 tsp honey or coconut nectar

Break down the cauliflower in a food processor until it's the size of rice grains. Grind up the sesame and coconut. Stir everything together in a bowl. Save leftovers for sushi the day after tomorrow.

Cauliflower Rice & Curry

Kale Caesar Salad

Serves two

Presoak seeds 2 hrs, takes 20 mins to make

100g kale

4 romaine lettuce leaves

2 tbsp olive oil

Pinch salt

1 cup (120g) sunflower seeds

1 clove garlic

10g fresh dill

1 lime, juiced

Pinch salt

1 cup (250ml) water

2 tbsp capers

6 sun-dried tomatoes

2 tbsp walnuts

2 flax crackers

Presoak your sunflower seeds for at least a couple of hours in advance. It helps with digestibility if you soak your walnuts as well, although this isn't essential, or you can buy activated walnuts from us at Raw Living.

Tear your kale into tiny pieces. Massage it with the olive oil and a pinch of salt to help break down the fibres. Put it in your salad bowl. Tear 4 romaine leaves into bite-sized pieces as well, and add those to the bowl. To make the dressing, drain the sunflower seeds, juice the lime, and blend everything up together until smooth. Pour it over your salad and mix thoroughly (you may well have excess dressing which you can reserve for another day, it makes a wonderful dip or spread). Mix in the capers, sun-dried tomatoes and walnuts, and serve into bowls or plates. Garnish with broken chips of flax crackers. Turmeric Butter (page 62) for a real feast.

Sea Spaghetti in Pesto

Serves 2

50g sea spaghetti

Pesto:

50g (1/2 cup) shelled hemp seeds

125 ml (1/2 cup) olive oil

1/4 t salt

50g basil, fresh

1/2 lemon, juiced

1 tsp coconut sugar

1 tsp chlorella powder

Soak your sea spaghetti overnight, for 12 hrs at least, or longer. You can use the pesto recipe given, or use the leftover sour cream from a few days ago. It also works with marinara.

To make the pesto, get the freshest basil you can. Pesto is all about good quality basil. Remove any large stems, and put it in the blender with all the other ingredients. Don't be scared of the chlorella! It adds a ton of nutrients, great colour, and you will barely taste it. Pesto keeps well, if you don't use it all, transfer it to a glass container and store in the fridge. It's great in nori rolls or spread on crackers as well as a salad dressing.

Pesto

Sunflower Stuffed Peppers

(Original recipe in Eat Smart, Eat Raw)

Serves 2

Takes 15 mins (plus pre-soaking)

150g (5 oz) mixed vegetables eg carrot, celery, broccoli

25g (1 oz) parsley

60 g (2 oz) sunflower seeds, soaked 2-4 hrs

1 tbsp flaxseed oil

1/2 lemon, juiced

1 tsp tamari

1 tsp ground cumin

Pre-soak the seeds for a couple of hours. Choose your favourite vegetables, or have a look what's leftover in your fridge and use up the odd bits of pepper, tomato, carrot or cucumber that always seem to accumulate. Put the seeds in first and give them a quick blitz. Then add the veg and parsley and blitz again. Next, add the oil, lemon juice, tamari, and cumin, and mix for minute until it's evenly mixed into one creamy mass. Leave a bit of texture in it, it's nicer left a bit crunchy rather than completely smooth.

Cut the peppers in half and scoop out the seeds. Spoon the pâté into the peppers. If you have a dehydrator, you can put them in for a couple of hours to soften the peppers and bring out the flavours.

Instant Kelp Noodles

(Original recipe in Eat Smart Eat Raw)

Serves two

Takes 15 mins

100g (4 oz) mushrooms

1 red pepper

1 pkt (340g) kelp noodles

1 lemon, juiced

1 tbsp tamari

2 tbsp tahini

60 ml (1/4 cup) extra virgin olive oil

125 ml (1/2 cup) water

1 tbsp apple cider vinegar

1 tsp smoked paprika

Open the kelp noodles, rinse them well in warm water, and cut them up with scissors. Put them in a bowl with the tamari and lemon juice, and marinate while you make the sauce. It helps to soften them if you massage them in the marinade. Fine slice the mushroom and pepper, and put them in a large bowl. In a separate smaller bowl, mix up the tahini, olive oil, water, and apple cider vinegar with a whisk or a fork. Stir in the smoked paprika. Drain the kelp noodles (I reserve the marinade and use it for a cracker batter or salad dressing another day). Add them to the bowl with the vegetables and the dressing, mix it all together, and there you have it! Barely takes longer than a pot noodle, and infinitely more tasty.

Snacks

These might well be your favourite part of the day! The wonderful thing about raw vegan snacks is as well as being absolutely super nutritious, they are the most delicious treats you have ever tasted. This is the part of your daily menu that will have everyone else super jealous of what you are eating. Double up if you want to share, and entice people onto the raw path with you. Sauerkraut salad and green juice aren't everyone's cup of tea, but few people turn their nose up at raw chocolate and blueberry pie.

Shortbread

Makes 12 pieces

Takes 20 mins with 1 hr setting time

(Original recipe is Tarts for the Tart in Raw Magic)

175 g or 1 1/2 cups coconut oil

200 g or 2 cups buckwheaties

200 g or 2 cups lucuma powder

100 g or 2/3 cup cane juice crystals

250 ml or 1 cup water

Melt the coconut oil in a heatproof bowl stood in simmering water, it will take about 5 mins. Grind the buckwheaties to a flour, and transfer them to a mixing bowl. Stir in the lucuma and cane juice crystals. Add coconut oil and water, and mix it all together until you have a dough. Set in a cake tin lined with foil or silicon mold. Sets in the fridge in an hour. If you're ready to be really fancy, look up my recipe for Zillionaire Shortbread online. This involves a caramel layer and a chocolate topping, and is well worth the extra effort. Just Google "Zillionaire Shortbread Kate Magic" and it will pop up.

Chia Cookies

Makes 25 cookies

Soaking time 4hrs, dehydrating time 18 hrs

125 g (1 cup) chia seeds

125 g (1 cup) flax seeds

750 ml (3 cups) water

50 g (1/2 cup) cacao powder

50 g (1/2 cup) lucuma

50 g (1/2 cup) cane juice crystals

50 g or (1/2 cup) raisins

Soak the chia and flax seeds together in the water for at least four hours, preferably overnight. When you are ready, stir all the other ingredients into the soaked seeds; this will take a few minutes of patience. When you're satisfied it's all fully mixed, spread them onto two dehydrating sheets. Dry for 12 hrs, then score into five by five (25 biscuits on each sheet), flip and dry for six hours more. The end result should be moist and irresistible. If you're feeling really decadent, you can spread them with the chocolate spread recipe on page 61.

Trail Mix

Choose from:

Coconut chips

Cacao nibs

Goji berries

Mulberries

Yacon root

Incan berries

Longan berries

Bee pollen

Shelled hemp seeds

Raw chocolate buttons

Blueberry Pie

Makes 12 slices

Takes 45 mins, 1 hr setting time

2 cups (100g) coconut flakes

1 cup (60g) sesame seeds

1/2 cup (50g) goji berries

1 cup (100g) lucuma

1 tbsp honey

2 tbsp coconut oil

1/4 cup (60 ml) water

1 tbsp cinnamon

2 cups (250g) cashews (soaked 4-8hrs)

1 cup (125g) coconut oil

1 cup (250 ml) water

2 cups (250g) blueberries

1 tbsp purple corn extract

1/2 cup (90g) cane juice crystals

Grind the coconut flakes, sesame seeds, and goji berries together in a food grinder or high power blender. Then stir in the lucuma and cinnamon. When they are evenly mixed, add the honey and coconut oil. The coconut oil only needs to be pre-melted if it's very solid. If it's a little soft, you should be able to rub it in. Then add the water gradually until you have a firm ball of cookie dough. Press it into your pie dish, over the bottom and up the sides. A 9" silicon mould works best. If you don't have a silicon mould, line a spring form or loose bottom pie tin with aluminium foil or greaseproof paper.

Pop it in the freezer to chill while you make the filling. Melt your coconut oil. Drain your cashews, and put them in the blender with the melted coconut oil and water. Blend until smooth and then add the blueberries, purple corn and cane juice crystals. Blend again, and then pour out into your pie crust. Pop in the freezer to set in 30 mins, or in the fridge in a few hours.

Blueberry Pie

Raw Chocolate

Makes 20 servings

Takes 15 mins, plus setting time 1hr

100g cacao liquor (paste)

25g cacao butter

50g cane juice crystals

Grate the cacao liquor and butter first to make the next step easier. Melt everything together by putting the ingredients in a heat-proof bowl, and standing it in gently simmering boiling water for 5-10 mins. Add your favourite flavourings eg essential oils or Medicine Flower Extracts. You can also add a teaspoon of your favourite superfood, eg Ashwagandha or He Shou Wu. Once it's liquid, pour into silicon moulds and set in the freezer for 30 mins-1 hr. Store in the fridge or freezer.

Candy

Makes 30 pieces

Takes 10 mins, 1 hr setting time

150g coconut oil

150g lucuma powder

100g raisins

Melt the coconut oil, by putting it in a heat-proof bowl, and standing it in a pan of gently simmering water. It should melt within 5 minutes. Remove it from the heat, and stir in the lucuma and raisins. Pour it into silicon molds, set in freezer for 30 mins to 1 hr. You can flavour this however you choose. I use 5 drops Medicine Flower Rum Extract to make Rum & Raisin, which is very popular! It also works well with food grade peppermint or orange essential oil e.g. Doterra. I would do 5 drops of peppermint or rum flavour, or 10 drops of orange.

Candy

Equipment lists

Measuring spoons

Measuring cups

Kitchen scissors

A selection of large and small bowls

Ceramic knife & wooden chopping board

Silicon moulds for chocolate & candy making

A cafetiere or teapot with a built-in strainer

A Mylk bag – for Mylks and juices

A spiralizer

Cake tin lined with foil or silicon moulds for cakes

Heatproof bowls for heating sauces/melting chocolate

Some airtight containers for storing leftovers in the fridge – I prefer glass

A good water filter is essential. The most basic option is to buy a jug filter from the High Street and energise it yourself with rose quartz crystals, affirmations, or energizing devices such as the Personal Harmonisers we have on the website from CIR.

A dehydrator will help with the preparation of the cereals, cookies, breads, crackers, kale crisps and falafel. If you don't have one, it's not essential, you can purchase these items ready-made from Raw Living or a good health food store. Where possible, I have given recommendations.

A high power blender will be invaluable, and there are so many to choose from nowadays. At the bottom end of the budget scale you have the Nutribullet. This works well but the disadvantage is you can only do small quantities. I currently have an Optimum G2.6 which I am really happy with, which we sell on **RawLiving.eu**. I also have a Thermomix which I absolutely love, and I would say if you have the budget and you are considering it, it is most definitely a purchase you won't regret

Shopping lists

This may seem like a big list! But take a good look through it, hopefully you will have a fair amount of it in your cupboards already. It makes sense to buy everything in larger quantities in the first week than keep buying small amounts throughout the month: you make your money go further this way, and save repeated trips to the shops.

Please remember the lunch and dinner recipes serve two, so take that into account when you are shopping for and preparing your meals.

I would recommend getting all the superfoods and groceries in for the entire month before you start. And then shopping for the fruit and veg from a local organic supplier at frequent intervals.

Week One:

Don't forget to also get the shopping in for your favourite dinner on Day 7.

Superfoods (all available from Raw Living)

1 kg shelled hemp seeds

1 kg lucuma

1 kg chia seeds

1 kg coconut oil

500g hand-cracked cashews

250g goji berries

250g cacao powder

100g cacao butter

100g maca

250g coconut chips

50g reishi extract

100g purple corn extract

100g Baobab

1 Eterniteea (loose tea)

1 Infiniteea (loose tea)

1 Gynostemma (loose tea)

1 jar tahini

1 tub lecithin

1 jar raw honey or coconut nectar (or both)

500ml extra virgin olive oil

250 ml hemp oil

250 ml flaxseed oil

250 ml raw apple cider vinegar

10 nori sheets

500g buckwheaties

2 x 250g Ecuadorian cane juice crystals

1 Magic Mix (or make your own trail mix)

1/2 oz Vanilla Medicine Flower Extract

Raw bread or crackers eg Wrawps, Raw Health (or make your own)

100g dulse flakes

100g turmeric powder

750g flaxseeds

100g almonds

500g sunflower seeds

100g whole hemp seeds

100g hazelnuts

250g sun-dried tomatoes

celtic sea salt

Groceries (all available from a good health food store)

500g sesame seeds

500g raisins

250g quinoa

250g millet

1 pkt rice cakes

1 pkt oatcakes

1 bag corn chips

1 tube wasabi

1 jar mustard

1 pot hummus

1 pkt Tempeh

500 ml tamari

250 ml balsamic vinegar

1 jar miso

1 pkt arame

small pkt cinnamon

small pkt chilli powder

small pkt cardamom pods

small pkt cayenne pepper

small pkt mixed dried herbs

1 jar pickled beetroot

20g psyllium powder

Fruit & Veg (recommended organic wherever possible)

6 lemons

1 grapefruit

3 limes

1 box fresh dates (eg Medjool)

350g blueberries (frozen will do if they are not in season)

9 cucumbers (I buy by the box!)

4 head celery

2 lettuce

600g kale

100g rocket

250g baby leaf spinach

5 avocados

1 kg tomatoes

2 red onions

750g carrots

500g beetroot

600g broccoli (2 heads)

2 cauliflower

1 sweet potato

2 potatoes

5 red pepper

1 cabbage (red or white)

1 small butternut squash

1 courgette

1 fennel

50g parsley

25g basil

100g alfalfa sprouts

100g fresh ginger root

1 bulb garlic

lime leaves

lemongrass

1 fresh red chilli pepper

Week Two:

Don't forget to add the ingredients for your drinks – teas, Mylks and juices. Also you'll need the ingredients for Dinner on Day 14.

Superfoods

100g turmeric powder

1 jar kimchi

Groceries

1 pkt gluten-free pasta

1 jar yellow curry paste

250g sesame seeds

150 ml sesame oil

150 ml rice vinegar

Fruit & Veg

250g fresh fruit of your preference

3 lemons

3 avocados

500g tomatoes

1 yellow pepper

1 red pepper

2 cucumbers

500g carrots

1 celery

1 small white or red cabbage

1 red onion

2 romaine lettuce

200g baby spinach leaves

250g new potatoes

250g broccoli

4 parsnips

100g rocket

100g pak choi

100g cherry tomatoes

100g chestnut mushrooms

2 courgettes

100g alfalfa sprouts

25g basil

50g ginger

Week Three:

Once again, don't forget to add the ingredients for your drinks – teas, Mylks and juices. Also you'll need the ingredients for Dessert on Day 21.

Superfoods

2 x 500g oats
250g shelled hemp
1 jar sauerkraut
250g buckwheaties
500 ml extra virgin olive oil
1 pkt kelp noodles
1 jar tahini
1 pkt raw crackers or bread (or make your own)
2 jar olives
500g walnuts
1 jar pumpkin seed butter

Groceries

Small pkt cumin

Fruit & Veg

1 courgette
1kg tomatoes
250g cherry tomatoes
2 yellow pepper
1 red pepper
7 lemons
5 avocados
750g carrots
1 cauliflower
1 cucumber
250g broccoli
50g green beans
2 romaine lettuce
200g baby leaf spinach
200g kale
2 red onion
1 celery
100g chestnut mushrooms
100g alfalfa sprouts
100g parsley
100g basil
25 g coriander
25g mint
1 red chilli pepper
50g ginger

Week Four:

I'm sure by now you're going to remember the ingredients for your teas, Mylks and juices! Also you'll need the ingredients for Lunch and Dinner on Day 22, and your final Feast on Day 28.

Superfoods

100g sea spaghetti

100g chlorella powder

1 jar olives

1 pkt crackers (or make your own)

1 pkt Wrawps

1 jar Rawmesan

1 pkt kelp noodles

1 pkt Magic Mix (or ingredients for your own trail mix)

120g sunflower seeds

1 pkt wakame

1 jar kimchi

Groceries

1 jar capers

Fruit & Veg

1 apple

3 lemons

1 avocado

1 cauliflower

3 tomatoes

4 carrots

3 red pepper

1 courgette

1 cucumber

1 romaine lettuce

1 lime

10g fresh dill

1 red chilli pepper

10g ginger

100g mung bean sprouts

250g chestnut mushrooms

100g baby leaf spinach

100g kale

25g parsley

Resources

Book List

Adaptogens by David Winston & Steven Maimes

Diet for a Small Planet by Frances Moore Lappe

Enzyme Nutrition by Edward Howell

Seven Health Secrets of the Hive by CH Robson

The PH Miracle by Dr Robert O Young

Conscious Eating by Gabriel Cousens

Cellular Awakening by Barbara Wren

Wild Fermentation by Sandor Ellis Katz

The Body Ecology Diet by Donna Gates

Raw by Juliano

Superfoods by David Wolfe

Lifefood Recipe Book by Annie Jubb

Spontaneous Evolution & Biology of Belief by Bruce Lipton

Molecules of Emotion by Candace Pert

The Hidden Messages in Water by Masaru Emoto

Survival into the 21st Century by Viktoras Kulvinskas

The Healing Powers of Pollen by Patrice Percie du Sert

Deadly Harvest by Geoff Bond

Earthing by Clint Ober

Love Without End by Glenda Green

Timeless Secrets of Health and Rejuvenation by Andreas Moritz

Eating on the Wild Side by Jo Robinson

Gut by Guilia Enders

Why We Sleep by Matthew Walker

Movie List

Vegucated

Forks Over Knives

Food Inc

Food Matters

Cowspiracy

Vaxxed

Fat Sick & Nearly Dead

Supersize Me

The Sacred Science

What the Health

Hungry for Change

The Bleeding Edge

The C Word

Heal

Root Cause

What's With Wheat

May I Be Frank

Fat Sick & Nearly Dead 2

Raw The Documentary

The Game Changers

More Books by Kate Magic

Eat Smart Eat Raw - simple and easy raw food recipes for beginners

Raw Living - raw food lifestyle and recipes for families

Raw Magic - superfoods guide and recipe book

The Empowered Woman - a holistic guide to understanding your hormones

Websites

RawLiving.eu
KateMagic.com
RawMagicAcademy.com
YouTube.com/wearerawliving
Mixcloud.com/katemagic

My instagram and twitter are **@katemagic**, Facebook is **@katelovemagic**.

Please note, all recipes are copyright © Kate Magic 2020. They are not to be reprinted or shared without prior permission, that includes blogs and other personal websites. Making these dishes to share with your friends and family is what they are intended for. However, if you intend to commercially profit from the recipes, by making them for resale or teaching them in classes, permission from the author needs to be granted first. We hope that this book has provided you with plenty of inspiration to make your own wonderfully original creations. If in doubt, please email **kate@rawliving.eu** for clarification, thank you.

Check out **KateMagic.com** for upcoming events. I hold classes, workshops, courses and retreats around the world; I hope you can join me at some point because as helpful as this book is, the information is so much more life-changing when you receive it in real life!

I also take private clients as my schedule permits. I offer in-person sessions from my home in central London, or video coaching. I have completed my 200hr Yoga Teacher Training with Stewart Gilchrist, Reiki Level 3 with Shaylini of The Sacred Self, and at the time of writing am studying Functional Nutrition with Andrea Nakayama. Private work includes looking at nutrition, diet and lifestyle solutions, using naturopathic detox techniques, and creating personally tailored affirmations with intention-setting and mindfulness tools to keep you motivated and inspired.

RawLiving.eu is your one stop shop for all your raw foods and superfood needs! We have been in business since 2002, and pride ourselves on curating a range of the very best high vibrational foods from around the planet, offering the best quality superfoods at the best possible prices, and providing exceptional customer service. If you don't already have an account, make sure you open one and receive £5 off your first order.

RawMagicAcademy.com is the site where you can find my beginners' classes in video format, and there are plenty more videos for you to browse on YouTube.

Lastly, as a DJ, you can catch me bi-weekly on Wednesdays 10am-midday on Soho Radio **(sohoradiolondon.com)** and the first Monday of the month 6-8pm on 1BTN.fm. Past shows can be found on my Mixcloud.

Email **kate@rawliving.eu** to enquire about booking coaching or an event (please note that I can't answer individual health queries this way).